It Takes a Naked Man
to Tell a Naked Story

IT TAKES A NAKED MAN
to Tell a Naked Story

STEVE MAZZA

It Takes A Naked Man to Tell a Naked Story

Copyright © 2013 Steve Mazza

ISBN-13:978-1-938886-96-6

ISBN-10:1938886968

ACKNOWLEDGMENTS

When I was a young man, my dad and I would sit up late nights watching TV. I recall a lot of wrestling, long before the WWF or any of today's pro wrestling associations. In conversation, Dad would always tell me I had lots of words in my head as I talked of my day's events. "Steve, you should write a book," he would say. So here I am writing a book. Dad passed away many years ago, but I have to say he is still my inspiration to write.

My mother was an artist, mostly doing still life studies and painting outdoor scenery whenever we went on family picnics. She took painting lessons at the same art institute I work for now. It gives me a coming-home feeling.

I like to tell stories to my friends; mostly jokes, fishing stories and my modeling job adventures. They always seem to enjoy my stories, which is another reason I thought perhaps a book was in order. To Bob and Lynn, close friends and supporters, thanks for your encouragement.

My brother and sister have both had outstanding careers in education and remain stellar examples of what good educators are all about. I like to feel I followed their example—even if I only contributed in a small way to the student learning process. Many thanks to Brian and Karen.

Thanks to all the teachers and staff at the community college, Jim and Jed in particular for providing a nurturing environment and tolerating my pushing the envelope. I feel very welcome to the fold and have made many friends.

Thanks to the complete staff at the art institute that offered my first opportunity to become a model. Thanks to Gregg, Steve, Ken, Chris, Annette and Jenna for your tutelage and embracing my modeling style. To all the students that have rendered my image in one form or another, you have been so accepting, gracious, and inspiring. Thanks and best wishes for your art careers.

Thanks most of all to my loving wife Patricia who put up with my crazy ideas for so long with little complaint and much tolerance. Not many would support a spouse with a job like this.

TABLE OF CONTENTS

THE ART OF HEATHER RYERSON

The cover picture of Steve in the chair was inspired by a "Bond" movie. This along with the illustration of "Stinky Feet" and the "Death Scene" are the works of Heather Ryerson, a friend and former student of classes I have modeled for. I am pleased to have her contribution to this book. The following is her very interesting bio.

Art has always been a love of Heather's, but she didn't take the primrose path to make it to her career. Heather helped her mother through a very long battle with breast cancer, ending with her mother's death when Heather was 20. Aside from having her life turned upside down and inside out, about 18 months later Heather began to notice a strange area of distortion in her vision. The same day she received a diagnosis of macular degeneration. The condition eventually developed in both eyes. After years of regular and painful treatment, her vision was finally stabilized. Heather was left with blind spots and distortions in her central vision, but could still focus and see almost normally with some effort.

Through these tribulations, art was always a peaceful place for Heather, even at points when she was legally blinded in one eye. She realized that if art kept her going then, it was clear that it was the only thing she could do with her life and that she had to be an artist. Heather and her husband worked together to allow her to start back to school with a major in Illustration at Mohawk Valley Community College in Utica, NY. She graduated with an AAS in Illustration at the top of her class, and earned enough in scholarships to transfer to Syracuse University to continue her studies in Illustration. She graduated from Syracuse University with a BFA in Illustration in May 2013.

Heather focuses on painting, both traditional and digital, for fantasy, sci-fi, and comic book work. She also enjoys the challenge and concept of editorial illustration work. Heather ideally would love to fully illustrate novels, as she is a voracious reader and gets a thrill from bringing the words of the authors to visual life.

BFA, Illustration, Syracuse University, Syracuse, NY 2013 AAS, Illustration, Mohawk Valley Community College, Utica, NY 2011

heather@ryersonillustration.com

www.HeatherRyersonIllustration.com

INTRODUCTION

I can't believe I'm watching "Dancing with the Stars" as I write this. But nowhere else on television could I find a better celebration of the human body as poetry in motion so beautifully choreographed to romantic music. This is exactly how I feel about figure drawing and figure painting in the classroom of art schools. It is a celebration of the human form. What better way could we find to record for all time the essence of mankind that our Creator gave to us? The muscle mass, tissue, bones and brains that make it all work in both a graceful and intelligent manner can be recreated on canvas and paper, and saved as a historical record of man's achievement. Bringing this creation to the art galleries of the world is to praise and honor the human race in all its magnificence and frailty.

What follows here is the author's discovery, late in life, of the joy of figure art and the contribution made by the nude model. Whether rendered as an action hero, secret agent or an athlete, his artistic image tells a "Naked Story" that can only be told by the man who lived it, the "Naked Man." Artistry and humor combine to bring you into the life of a senior citizen who finds that some decisions he made along the way will culminate in a classroom career like no other.

THE BEGINNING

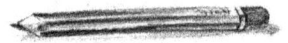

The night air is full of tension. It's quiet, but eerie like before a storm. Suddenly all hell breaks loose. The whistling of incoming rockets sends a chill up my back and my heart starts racing like there is no tomorrow. Light flashes. *Blam, boom, whoosh.* Flares go up and the sound of small arms fire is heard all over the perimeter. I didn't need to hear it, but someone yells "incoming" as if I didn't know what was happening, but none the less, it serves to confirm my worst fears: we are under attack!"

I roll out of my bunk, hit the ground and crawl on my belly to a bunker just 15 feet away. It's a long 15 feet as shrapnel whistles by my ear after a rocket lands nearby. That was close—too close for comfort. Everyone is scrambling for protection and setting up defensive gun positions. We are pinned down with heavy mortar and rocket fire for over an hour, and then the camp sirens switch to ground attack. Okay, now I'm really getting nervous. Truth be known, I was nervous for hours before. You see, I knew this was coming and yet I was still questioning the validity of the information I had at hand. It's January 30, 1968 and this is the Tet offensive of the Viet Cong in South Vietnam. I'm an intelligence analyst working with an undercover platoon that has the most accurate information on where the bad guys are and I give briefings daily to information officers that advise the infantry on "Charlie's" (the Viet Cong) locations.

Back in the hole I can smell the dirt. It's humid and the air is thick with smoke and the smell of gunpowder. Light flashes from explosions, giving brief illumination in the dark night like camera flashes with a big bang attached. I'm hot, sweaty, dirty and tired. This is like a story you read about someone else's life and you wonder if it's actually happening to you.

The Bell Ring

Suddenly a little bell goes off and I feel a chill all over. I'm a little disoriented, and as I come to my senses I realize I am totally naked and standing in the middle of a room surrounded by young people just staring at me. Oh my god, I was having a flashback to Vietnam while on the job at my art class. The bell was the timer for the drawing session and once again my mind has taken me out of the room to relive some part of my life.

My story might start off like an AA meeting. Hi, my name is Steve and I am a nude figure model. Maybe I should start the NMA (Nude Models Anonymous). If the room was full of other nude models I would get a standing applause, but I doubt you will ever see that happen. When I do tell people I am a nude model I usually see some form of shock and words like "you're a what?" A few that have had experience with the art community in one way or another have a much more understanding expression and sometimes even a knowing smile because they took a figure drawing class at some time. This book is inspired by those who have both love and understanding of my craft. Craft you say? Why, don't you just stand there and do nothing? Oh, my friends, for someone who takes this seriously, those are fighting words! There is nothing easy about being a nude model if you really have the intent of giving an artist the motivation to draw the best picture they can. Second, this is a unique craft that only a few brave souls are willing to even attempt. However, if you have a "life is a bowl of cherries" world view, then this could be just the ticket you were looking for.

The Job

I'm not going to talk very much about good art poses or even the etiquette of model and student relationships. This is much more about the humor, fun and satisfaction of working in the nude. Let me just whet your appetite first with a little story of being a nude model in a northern climate in winter. I'm from upstate New York—I mean like in the middle of the state just on the edge of the lake effect snow belt. We measure snow in feet up here, not inches, and temperatures can frequently be well below zero during midwinter.

I have modeled in winter for six years now and it does make an interesting if not challenging situation. Imagine you just took a shower and are rushing to get to class on a zero-degree day. So you throw something on without too much thought and jump into a totally frozen car after scraping the windshield of ice and pushing a foot of central New York snow off the hood so you can see the road. The windshield is taking too long to defrost so you can't see well and the roads are very slippery, both of which slow your commute and add to the pain of an already dropping body temperature.

When you arrive on campus the parking lot is slush and ice and you soak your running shoes because you left the winter boots where you couldn't find them in a hurry. Now you rush into a waiting class that needs to see your nude body from head to toe, even though it's shades of blue and covered in goose bumps. First, I run into my changing area which is the size of two phone booths, take off my clothes and grab a robe. I come out to the model stand, usually in the center of the room surrounded by up to 18 students. I'm elevated about one foot so they get a good view from just 6 to 8 feet away. *What am I doing here*, you ask yourself. And then you remember. *Oh yes, they pay me to do this.* Now where else could you have this much fun and get paid for it, especially after age 65?

I put a quartz box heater at my feet and between my legs if possible to warm those important areas (we men are always concerned about shrinkage) and just the ride to work would make a belly button that's normally an "outie" become an "innie." I try to picture a nice hot sun shining down with me lying on a beach and I'm getting a great tan even though there is snow on the ground outside. So now you are getting the idea, but before I go too far let's get back to the beginning. Just how did I get in this line of business anyway?

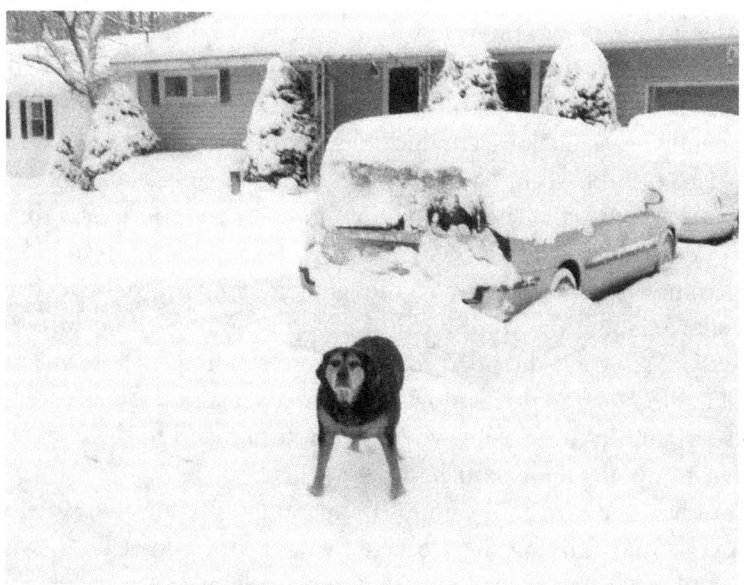

Diesel helping me dig out the cars

DECISIONS

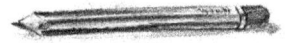

Where to begin? This is a story of where your life can lead you and how every turn seems to have a new road that you could follow forever, or at least until you get to the next turn. I say this because I have had many turns and many interests. Most of us think our lives are pretty mundane and we plod along doing the same thing every day. Do you remember your childhood? Ever recall thinking you would be a kid forever or what would it be like to be grown up and what would you do as a grown up?

Given my age and generation, a lot of this stuff seemed to be cut and dry. You went to school, even college, picked a career, found a spouse, got married, bought a nice house preferably with a picket fence around it and raised a family. Sound familiar? Maybe you're still in the beginning process, and if you are today, these values may be very different for you, but in each case I would tell you to stop and smell the roses, think about your choices, and take your time and enjoy. The ride will be much faster than you think and one day all of a sudden you're closer to the end than the beginning.

So I would say to you, don't just plod along; be energetic, vibrant, and creative in all you do and by all means work at something you enjoy and have fun. It's not so much about the money, it's about life, living and loving. The money will follow, so get the happiness part right first. My purpose is not to wax philosophical here, it's to stimulate your vision of life by sharing some of mine, and *hopefully* you will see some humor and enjoyment that could give you some impetus to take the next new turn in your world. That next turn could lead to something very unexpected. Now unexpected could be good, could be not so good, but you won't know if you don t take a look. I say at least take the look. What's the harm in looking?

Most of my working life, which started basically at 16, has been spent in the kitchen design and sales field. I took a course in high school that I really wasn't sure would be useful, but it turned out pretty good. Remember needing an elective course and you took a stab because it looked interesting? Well, one of my electives was drafting. You might call it mechanical drawing. I learned how to draw nuts and bolts, straight lines and curvy lines, perspective angles and so on. I even learned how to draw a long line without flattening one side of your pencil lead. (Oh well, if you must know it's rotating the pencil as you drag along a line. It takes some practice but makes a neat line when done right.)

My dad had a kitchen design business and I started there, drawing pretty pictures of kitchens so a customer could see how their new kitchen would look, and WOW, all of a sudden that elective drafting course came in real handy. Well, here we go, that was another turn in the road I spoke about. Taking drafting was a curiosity at first, but it turned out to be essential for my design career. I didn't know kitchen design would turn out to be a career at the time, but it has been for me for over 40 years. See, you just never know what will happen. Now, how I got into the family business was really another turn of events.

THE HAIRCUT

Lyndon Johnson was president in 1964 and had a daughter named Lynda Bird. At the same time there was a Marine First Lieutenant David LaFerve serving as an aide at the White House and, while at a garden party, a picture was taken of LaFerve dancing with Lynda Bird. LaFerve had a Mohawk haircut, which I thought was really cool. You know, that clean shave on both sides with a 2-inch-wide hair strip right up the middle and down to your neck? The hair strip itself was usually a brush cut about an inch to two inches high. Thinking that this was a really cool haircut, I decided to go to my Italian barber and ask him to give me one.

Now mind you I was 19 at the time and still living with parents that had house rules. Barbers of the time were timid to give you a non-traditional hair cut if your parents hadn't really approved. None the less, I managed to convince Joe the barber that it was fine. "After all, Joe, look at the paper. Here is the president's daughter seen with a guy wearing this Mohawk. How bad could it be?" Reluctantly, Joe agreed if I would not spread the word to all my friends about where I got it because he did not want a run on that haircut and be faced with a bunch of angry parents.

Oh, Joe, if you only knew that haircut turned out to be a career decision for me. You see, unknown to me, my dad had lined up a job for me at one of the local banks as a teller. When I went home for dinner that very same day my mother was in shock at the haircut before Dad even got home from the office. We all sat down for dinner and here comes Dad. Holy crap did he hit the ceiling. He then told me about the job prospect at the bank and told me not to even go for an interview with that haircut. "Gee, Dad, how about that bank with the Indian head logo instead?" I replied flippantly. Not a smart thing to say to Dad just then.

So there I was without a job for the summer break, and Dad was furious. Mom thought I needed a job anyway, so she suggested to Dad that he give me a job in his kitchen business. Bingo! I started with kitchens as a teenager and the rest is history, as they say.

Did you see this coming? There was that turn in the road again and a choice I made had a direct effect on a big part of my life. Imagine a haircut that became a career decision.

Who knows, if not for the haircut I may have spent my life as a banker. Mind you, the kitchen business turned out to be very interesting and rewarding in many ways. I got to meet many very nice people on a personal level by working in their homes. I learned a lot about tools and general home construction and repair. Consequently, I can fix almost anything in my own home, which is a good thing in today's world. Oh, and just for the record here, the Mohawk cut was a Hollywood invention used during the making of the movie *Drums along the Mohawk*. It was not a traditional cut for the Mohawk tribe.

I love telling this story of how a haircut could be a career decision, but I have to admit a lot of water has passed under the bridge since this happened and in research I realized I had been telling the story wrong, You see, I knew that Lynda Bird Johnson had met a marine that she ultimately married. That was Marine Captain Charles Robb who later became U.S. Senator Robb from Virginia. I had remembered seeing the picture of a Marine with Lynda with that Mohawk and assumed it was Robb. Not being sure, I needed to do some research.

Working late one night I made the internet acquaintance of Jeff Malet a photographer from Washington D.C. I emailed Jeff at 1 a.m., asking if he could suggest a way to find this picture, and went to bed.

When I got up the next morning, I found seven emails from Jeff, sent to me between 2 a.m. to 3:30 a.m., which let me know that Jeff had done research for at least an hour and a half and in fact found my original picture with explanation that the marine in the picture was actually David LaFerve. Lynda had not met Robb until late 1966 after he had served in Vietnam. Interesting to this story are two coincidences. One, Laferve was from Latham N.Y. just an hour from where I grew up and still live. Second, I went to Vietnam just after Captain Robb came home. So it is with special thanks to Jeff Malet that I now have the correct story revolving around that silly haircut.

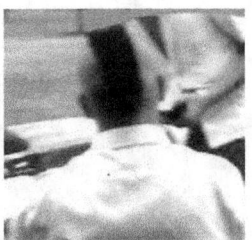

The haircut

THE ARMY

I was new to the kitchen business when I got an invitation from "Uncle Sam" that I wasn't really expecting. I was a part-time student going to night school at the local community college and working days in Dad's kitchen business. Those were the draft days and to be a full-time student you needed a certain number of credit hours to keep student status. Dropping one course put me just under that mark. It only took about two weeks and I had a draft notice. Well here comes another choice to make. Do you accept the draft call and take pot luck for the type of field the government will put you in or should you enlist for an extra year and get to pick your field?

I had a friend, Phil, from high school who was in the same spot, so we decided to enlist on the buddy plan they had at the time that would let you and your friend stay on assignment together. In those days James Bond movies were all the rage and I was sure I wanted to be a secret agent. After all, look at all those pretty girls Bond was having fun with. Naturally, I enlisted to get my choice and Phil did the same. Interestingly, the secret agent schools were a secret—not even known to the recruiters.

"You start here son, in Army intelligence school, and then you can transfer later," they told me. I can tell you that was a used car salesmen approach to get your signature. No offense to car salesmen, I've done that too. What you will learn first at Army Intel school is subjects that deal with combat intelligence and during a conflict or war like Vietnam, there is only one place they will send you with that training. You guessed it, right into the middle of it. Gee Steve, good choice you made there.

First you have to get through basic training, which Phil and I were doing together at Fort Bragg in North Carolina. After almost graduating I get pneumonia and hospitalized. Phil graduates without me and we are then split up. I'm 22 years old at this point and as many veterans can attest, this is a fast growing up experience. My first duty call was actually Hawaii and I figured I would be surfing and going out with college girls in no time. I had a friend with me that I met in training school who was from Indiana and a great college swimmer, or so he told me. He was really excited by our prospects in Hawaii. Well, we both got shipped to Vietnam after two weeks on Oahu. No college girls for us.

After arriving in Saigon, we found different assignments and split up and never saw each other until the day we left for home. I was in the southern zone and Tim went to the northern zone. Meanwhile, Phil ended up in the central highlands. All three of us were doing different intelligence missions.

My mission was tracking enemy troop movements by locating their tactical radios. The theory was that a unit is never more than a few kilometers from its radio operator. They knew we could track their radios by airborne radio direction finders, so their radio operators would leave a unit to make their scheduled transmissions to the other combat units and headquarters. Each day I worked with aircraft hunting those radios down and I would put a pin in a map to show locations that we could develop a history of and watch where they were going. My particular expertise as an analyst was to know the players and where they were going. Once a day or more, if necessary, I would report this info to the captain of our platoon, who in turn would brief the intelligence officer of our attached combat division. Lucky me, I was doing briefings for the 1st Infantry, also known as "The Big Red One," an Army division with a serious history—including the landing at Normandy in WWII.

This was pretty heavy stuff for a young man, and the pressure was on to be accurate. Lives were at stake and frequent combat missions and air strikes were planned with the info from my unit.

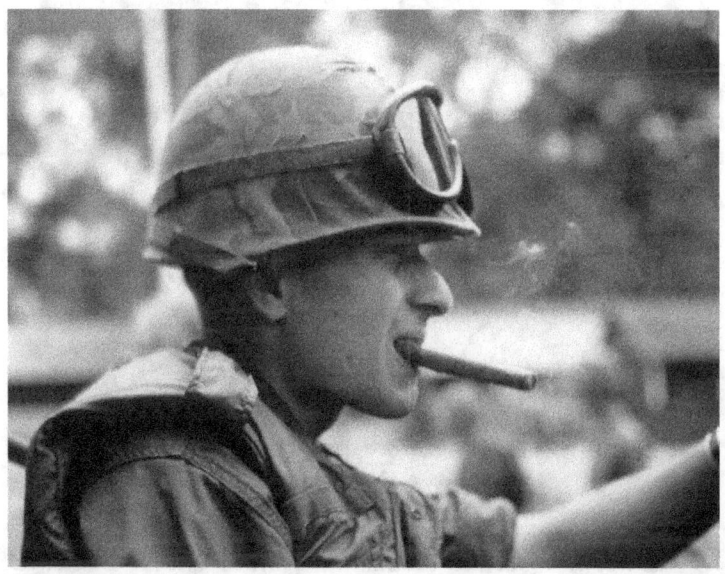

Steve on Convoy

We were in place under cover names, and not even our own troops, with exception of a few officers, knew what we really did. The mission gave me purpose day by day. That and letters from home got me through what could have been a disaster. Many of those letters and even audio tapes were from my parents, brother, sister and friends from church, and one girl in particular. Bee, I will call her, was my Uncle Rick's niece from Long Island. She came to visit my uncle one summer during my last year in high school and my uncle asked me to entertain her while she visited as we were close in age. I have to say there was electricity from the start, but we were young and nothing real serious was going to happen at that age, given the distance between us.

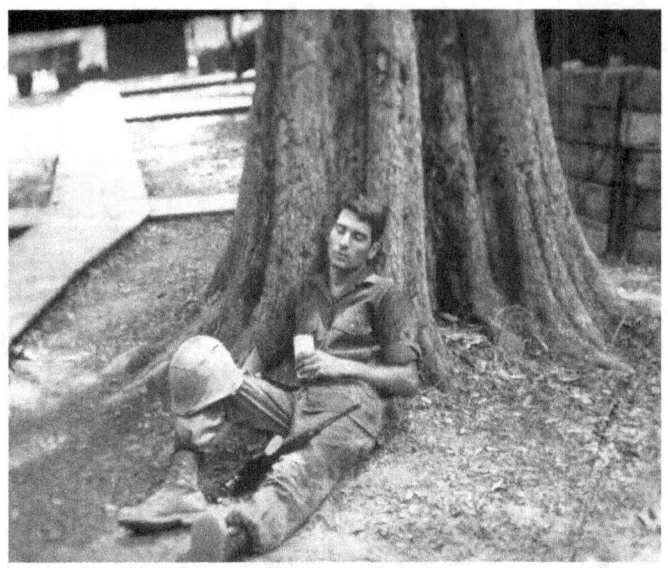

Getting some well-deserved rest

So fast forward back to Vietnam. My uncle sent me a letter telling me that Bee's brother, whom I had also met once, was in Vietnam and maybe I could look him up. Well, that seemed like looking for a needle in a hay stack, but when I went to my postmaster and asked where that coded address was, he laughed and pointed down the camp road. Sure enough, I found Junior, as they called him, sitting on his bunk in a tent. We had a nice talk and he told me Bee wasn't seeing anyone and perhaps I should write to her. Well, I did and the letters and tapes started flowing on a regular basis. She had a thick Long Island accent that when you played her tapes on those old reel-to-reel portable tape players just came out pure sexy. Those tapes got played over and over and sure helped pass the time. Thanks, Bee.

My unit commander was a captain and West Point graduate. A pretty sharp guy that took a liking to me and asked me to join him at the Pentagon assignment he was soon leaving for. I agreed to look him up when I got back and we would talk about it.

After being almost blown up more than once, I felt blessed to be able to go home without a scratch. The day I left Vietnam I saw Tim once again and was glad he made it, also. We hugged, shared some stories and boarded different planes never to see each other again. Phil actually signed on for a second tour, but we caught up after we both left the Army. We still live just a few miles apart and talk once in a while. Phil's sister Alyce and I have the same exact birthday and we all grew up in the same neighborhood, and this year we are going to our 50th high school reunion. How time flies.

I came home to what seemed like a hero's welcome, although I'm certainly not a hero, but family and friends that are just happy to see you in one piece certainly make you feel like one. The flight back to the states took its second fuel stop in Anchorage, Alaska. Those international flights make you want to take a stretch at any opportunity, so I went out and walked the terminal for a bit. I was in uniform and it didn't take but a few minutes and a couple stopped me to ask where I was coming from. I explained I just hit stateside coming in from Vietnam. Well I need to tell you this was a very emotional moment for me when complete strangers and the first people I was to meet said "welcome home, son." Those words seem so simple and yet so profound after what I had been through, I could have kissed them both. It still makes me tear up over 40 years later.

The next leg of the flight took me to San Francisco where my cousin Joy and her husband Harold picked me up. Joy had worked at a military lab doing research on malaria, and knew enough to scare me about the dangers of insect-infested jungles. I got her lecture on that before going to Vietnam, so I am sure she was happy to see me on the return trip and healthy. They entertained me for a few days at their summer home on a lake just north of the Bay Area. I hadn't seen Joy since she was a West Coast gal, but it was great to see her and relax for a few days in a peaceful setting. What a delightful stop that was, but I was still anxious to get all the way home.

I did go see Bee when I got back to New York and it was pretty steamy I must say, but alas, the timing was just not right and once again we parted ways. We have since reconnected in the electronic age with Facebook, and it's nice to be able to share life stories.

After a nice long rest, on my return I was stationed at Arlington Hall Station in Arlington, Virginia. It was here the Army decided to give me a nice clean desk job, so they sent me to a filing and correspondence course to prepare. This is where I met Patricia, a blonde, Italian protestant. (Most Italians have dark hair and few are protestants.) I figured that combination was unique enough that I had to investigate. One of my methods of testing a relationship at that time was to double date with my friend Ron and his then-fiancée Ann. I had met Ron in Vietnam and we hit it off quite well and stayed in touch on return as we had been placed fairly close together, though always on different posts. He was a real easygoing type with a great country boy smile and sense of humor.

The first time Ron and I went on a double date he gave me a big "Oh no," on my date choice and I trusted his judgment, so that was the last date with that gal. Well, I didn't really need him to point out the error of my ways, you see I had just met her the night before in a really dark bar. Being that I was just back from Vietnam a short time and really looking to fill my date book, the darkness did not dissuade me. In the bar this gal had a guy with her and I waited till he went to the bathroom, and then I sat in his seat at the bar next to her and introduced myself as a prospective new suitor. I think it took about two minutes to get her phone number. Maybe that should have been a clue. Well, it was darker than I thought in that bar because when I went to pick her up for our first date I did not recognize her at all and I am certain she could see the disappointment on my face. We went out with Ron and Ann to an ice cream place and the girls got out to go order for us. It was then that Ron exclaimed to me "Where did you find this one?" Enough said. That was our only date .

On the next double date with Ron and Ann I had Patricia with me and we went to the same ice cream place. Once again the girls got out to order and this time Ron turns to me and says, "Much better." I didn't really need Ron to tell me this one was a keeper and in fact we are still together after 45 years. We have two great children and six wonderful grandchildren.

DISCOVERING NUDE LIFESTYLES

I returned to the kitchen business and spent over 40 years in that field in different capacities from retail sales to sales rep to business owner. While a sales rep in upstate N.Y., I got to travel daily in many rural parts of the state. As an avid fisherman, this was perfect for me and my love of the outdoors. Often instead of taking a hotel room for the night I would stay in a campground that would be near a good fishing spot. While looking at the New York State campground guide one day I discovered one called a "full tan club." There, in small print, was the word "Nudist." Oh boy! That sounded interesting to me for some reason. I never was a modest person, not then or now. It would be discovery time for me and with all that travel time on the job, it was perfect.

One warm summer night I found myself in Cortland, New York which was just a stone's throw from the little village of Moravia. It was near there I found my first really obscure nude campground. Yippee! *Free at last, free at last* kept ringing through my head. Now this would be a different freedom than Dr. King had in mind and I certainly don't mean to belittle his mantra, it just seemed to be a neat phrase for my purpose here. Ahh, shedding the clothes in a country setting with no one waiting to arrest you for exposure was just a giddy thought. The campground just happened to be on the end of Licke Street (pronounced "lick").

This would be my first really grownup nude outdoor experience, besides some skinny dipping of course. I turned off of Licke Street onto a dirt road and maybe a half mile in I saw the campground sign. My heart rate increased and I became very nervous. The interior sign past a gate directed me to the office and also warned me that I was entering a nude environment. That would turn most people around right there, but not me.

I pulled up to park near the office sign and a woman steps out to meet me and invites me in to chat a bit before signing the camp register. Oh, did I mention, not just a woman, a rather full figure totally nude woman. Okay, there is no doubt I'm feeling quite awkward here because I'm dressed and she is nude. I'm invited to sit at the family table as this is both the manager's home and office, and it's dinner time. So there I sat for what I was thinking would be the inquisition of all inquisitions and Carol, my new found nude lady manager, sits to finish dinner and try to set me at ease. Carol has really large breasts and her key set on a leather lanyard is totally hidden between them. How do I know this? I'm staring, of course, because this is all new to me. Little did I know that many years later I would be a nude artist model and my decision to camp here was actually on-the-job training. You see, here we go again, what simple decisions can do to affect the sands of time in our own lives.

Perhaps I forgot to mention that I am married at this point, so seeing a pair of breasts shouldn't be shocking, but in truth I was a real late bloomer and had little experience with women prior to getting married. I married shortly after getting back from Vietnam, but that is a whole other story. Now I'm thinking I better not tell the wife yet that I'm staying overnight nude with a whole bunch of other nude people .

Carol sets me at ease with the rules of nude campgrounds and lets me pick a site to set up my tent for the night. The rules are pretty simple. Clothing is actually optional on your first visit, but if you do take them off you need to have a towel to sit on their furniture for hygiene reasons. No sexy clothing allowed, like a bikini, that would be considered provocative.

After setting up my little tent, I took off my clothes and tried not to look like a tourist in New York City, gawking at every tall building. The camp has lots of country acreage with a pond and walking trails, not to mention a pool, hot tub and sauna, so naturally I went to explore. Holy cow, I'm taking my first fully nude walk in what seemed to be a public environment, even though it is rural. Walking up a country lane past some camping trailers, I come to an open field where someone is cutting the grass on a riding mower that is approaching me. This person is definitely not my next door neighbor from home, as I can immediately see a pretty young lady, with you guessed it, not a stitch on.

What a great way to cut the grass, I was thinking. Hell no, that is not what I was thinking! It was more like, *where can I hide because she is stopping to talk to me.* She is a regular here and can easily see I'm a visitor, so she is friendly and welcoming. I on the other hand am feeling really weird, but I'm trying to feel normal and all is calm in "Neverland." I really wish those perky young breasts weren't staring at me. She tells me there is an evening campfire chat and I'm thinking what a good way to get immersed in this. After all, it would be dark for a campfire, and no one would be staring at me with night vision glasses. So I give a "thank you," and continue on my hike as I wave goodbye, while admiring that nice tractor she is riding. I must admit this walking around nude with the sun and breeze on your skin is very liberating, and I can begin to feel more relaxed as the time goes by.

More Exploring

That evening I was prepared to brave a group meeting so I started my way in the direction I was given for the campfire. Apparently it was a nightly thing to share stories of the day and meet newcomers like myself. I came to the spot where a few were gathered. They must have been regulars because they knew I was a visitor and started introductions. Now as the rules go, it's first name only since most nudists don't want to advertise to the world who they are. I can tell you this, though—they are your kid's school teacher, your friendly airline pilot and even your plumber.

There are about a dozen around the fire, but that seems like 200 when you are nude. I'm a mixer normally, but it took me a bit longer under my new name "Naked Steve." The folks that are regulars here were very friendly, and genuinely they try to make you feel at home. Let me see now, raise your hands readers, how many are nude at home right now? Not too many I see. This book has the latest technology to let the author see how the reader is reacting. Just kidding, no reason to hide for those of you that are nude.

Even in summer the evening temperatures in upstate New York may not be best for being nude outdoors, but I'm not going to look like the new guy unless everyone else gets dressed, so goose bumps and all I tough it out, and get as close to the campfire as I can without turning into a crispy critter.

Sleeping can be chilly in a tent but no one can see me, so I am covering up to be comfortable till sunrise. I slept in a bit, till my bladder told me it's wake up time. First thought in the morning of course, is get to the bathroom, but in a nudist camp it's not quite the same as at home. I crawl out of my little two person tent that is really just big enough for one and a phone book, and start my way to the bath house.

Now I'm looking for the men's entrance when I recall there isn't one, it's one entrance for both sexes because this is a unisex bath house. I'm sure this will be interesting, if not weird, the first time around. Sure enough, here is my cute little lawn cutting friend totally nude in front of the vanity mirror doing her eye makeup. I say good morning as she smiles and recalls our meeting the day before and asks how I slept. "Chilly in the tent, miss, but I survived and I'm looking forward to another summer day." So I set my toiletry bag on the counter and pulled out my shaving stuff. You see I had no pockets. I start shaving, trying not to cut my throat while those breasts are staring at me again, only this time they are right next to me as well as facing me in the mirror. Without steady hands, it could be a potentially disastrous situation indeed.

What a nice young lad, y I'm thought, but knew I'd better jump in that cold shower and finish getting ready to go back on the road. The bathroom had several toilet stalls as well as shower stalls, but no gender signs anywhere. So it's really weird to take a shower with a curtain for a door, and then come out nude to a room that may have women in it. This time just the young lady and I are sharing this room, but I would find out later that it was a community bathroom that the whole campground shared. Life in that campground was certainly interesting. Truth is, I really enjoyed my stay and it would be the first of many, as my travels would bring me that way often.

As a footnote to this camp story, I will share with you how the company I worked for questioned my camping expenses. They thought perhaps I was charging recreation time when I should have been working. I asked if they would rather have a fifty dollar hotel bill or a ten dollar camping fee and suddenly there was no problem. It was some time before they actually learned some of my stays were in "nude" campgrounds, but outside of a few jokes there was no condemnation.

Several years later I would meet Carol the camp manager and her husband in a new campground location that they had purchased for themselves. I had taken a different job with another company in a fixed location about three hours from home. It was a kitchen selling job in a lumber company and I wasn't sure if it would turn out to be a long-term opportunity, so I was seeking a rental living situation till I was sure. This would mean commuting weekends to home.

I was not able to quickly find a suitable rental so I looked farther out of town, even looking at campgrounds. It was then I ran into Carol and Cap, as they called her husband. At this time they were the owners of a nude campground near Candor, N.Y. This turned out to be a fortunate meeting for me as I would end up taking a campsite and staying for several months. Now I would really get the total nude living experience.

Most of us go to a job location daily to perform whatever our job task is. It could be sales, clerical or manufacturing, but the fact remains it becomes rather routine until the day is over and then we return home. Even home can be routine. Pull in the driveway, walk to the front door, check the mail box, insert keys and open the door. Maybe your spouse or kids are home so certainly there is a greeting and "how was your day dear?" Now let's get out of those work clothes no matter what type they are because relaxation comes with a change in clothes that signal the work day is over. I have done all this for many years, but this particular year would be different.

I was working for the first time in a home center with a kitchen department. I would work daily with new customers who were shopping for kitchen cabinets and most frequently would need a design for their new kitchen. Spending hours of consultation time and design time is not physically demanding but mentally can be very fatiguing. I had several co-workers in the kitchen department, all of whom were women. Some had been friends for years from my sales rep days. Only two, Wendy and Patty, knew that I would be going home to a nude campground every night. These gals were trusted friends and found it quite amusing. No, they did not ask to come visit, ha ha.

Now, here is the difference in the coming home part. I drove to a small village which was rural to begin with and then took a dirt road to an even more rural location with a gate that warned you of entering a nude campground. Upon entering you would normally sign in at the office, but regulars or seasonal members drove straight to their trailers or, in my case, a tent. My relaxation had already started with the rural drive and when I entered the park I became surrounded by trees and rolling lawns, and the serene and peaceful feel of nature abounds. I am not changing my clothes, I am taking them off completely and going for a walk through the woods or joining some friends at the clubhouse, all of whom are equally nude. Definitely not the same as pulling in my driveway. What's missing of course is the family, but I would need to put that aside till we figured out what would be best for us all in the long term.

I had set my tent up securely nestled in some trees next to a green lawn area. Inside I had what comforts I could make feel like home, but bare bones for sure: a cot with an air mattress, sheets and covers rather than a sleeping bag. I did have camp electricity, so lights, a small fridge and a gas heater for cool nights were my comforts. Magazines would be my entertainment. Signals were weak so far out in the country, so there was no TV or radio.

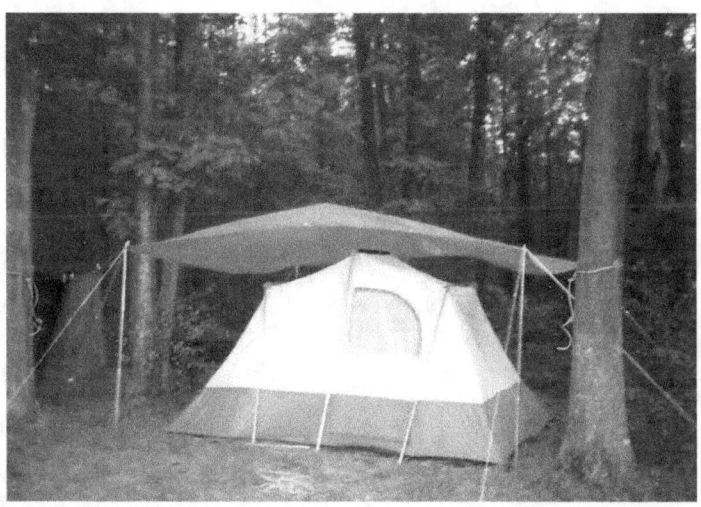

Campsite

My choices for leisure entertainment would be different than yours at home. If I chose to talk to my neighbors they were few and far between, and almost always nude. Imagine going to the fence to talk to your neighbor and they are nude. In some cases perhaps you would enjoy that, but most of us would probably agree that is not a sight we would embrace easily. At the campground, however, there is a very different feel. We expect people to be nude and if you were dressed, people would wonder why. Meeting places would include a large hot tub that would hold about eight, or the clubhouse with TV and a snack bar. There is also an outside swimming pool, and a pond with canoes and a beach area. Nature trails allow for walking the forested park dotted with campsites in both wooded and open grassy areas. Just keep in mind everywhere you go you will run into naked people and none of them will bat an eye about the nudity.

I have to say it took me a while to get used to the nudity on a daily basis, but once I did, I became quite comfortable with it. My personal pleasures became the hot tub and long nature walks. The tub was so relaxing with its heated whirlpool action and often a nice conversation with another guest. Cap and Carol always made me feel welcome and would be there in a heartbeat if I needed any help. Campfires at night were another favorite, just as I had discovered at my earlier nude camp experience, but now it could be a nightly routine. This place brought me lots of peace and the comfort to be myself in a totally nude environment. I ended up staying even after the camp season ended until my little heater was just not enough. In those last days I had the entire campground pretty much to myself, almost like my own little piece of paradise.

RUNNING

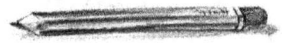

I have always had an interest in running for sport and exercise. I started in grade school with sprinting. I was pretty thin and lite in those days, probably about 120 lbs. One hundred yards would be my preferred distance then. I can remember my older brother, Brian, coming to an all-city championship back in the day when you had an elementary grade school K through eight every ten blocks or so. We had at least five in our city, so it made for a lot of competition at a track meet. Sure, any kid would love to show off in front of family or friends, so I was really happy to see Brian show up at the meet. I had just finished winning my heat when I saw Brian walking across the field. He looked like I was kidding him when I said I won, thinking it was the finals, but I explained it was my heat only and I got into the finals with that win.

"You did? Really?"

"Yes I did, big brother, so stick around for the finals."

He did, of course, and I was sure excited to have my own brother for a rooting section.

My coach was always on me about running with your eyes focused beyond the finish line so you would get to the finish at full speed. However, I had met the guy who was supposedly the fastest in the city. Charlie was actually a guy I knew from my church, so I had some trust

It Takes a Naked Man to Tell a Naked Story

in the advice he was giving me. I figured he was the best, so maybe he could help me too. Charlie's advice was to put your head down to reduce wind resistance and scoop your hands to push wind behind you as you swung your arms. Well, I made the mistake of trying something new with no testing and hit the finals with Charlie's form advice. Not good. When I was the fourth person to cross the finish line, my coach was all over me and yelling at the top of his lungs.

"What the hell was that, Steve? You killed your chances with that performance."

I explained what Charlie, the fastest kid, had told me and the coach of course was furious. Charlie's form was the worst way to run smooth in a sprint and had only negative effects. It turns out, Charlie was second on this day and he could have been much better if he had a proper clean sprint style. Head up, hands flat to slice air, not push it. Charlie had good intentions, he just didn't know any better and apparently his coach didn't correct him either so long as Charlie was winning. But, hey, making finals in a citywide championship wasn't too bad. Well now that my brother had seen me run he had gained a confidence in me that would lead to a match race on our block.

We use to play touch football right in the middle of the street in our neighborhood. Little and big kids all together. These were the days of lots of kids all on one block going to the same school. Mid to late 1950s was the day. A fella named Pete was older than me, and was reported to be the fastest around. We would race the distance between two telephone poles whenever someone questioned who was the quickest. One day that question came up during a football game in the street, and my brother decided it was high time for someone to challenge Pete. You guessed it, Brian told everyone his little brother could take Pete. Now the pressure is on for this kid to perform to big brother's challenge. To my own surprise, I actually beat Pete and felt I had redeemed myself from that All City Championship disaster, and Brian is happy to claim that his little brother is now the fastest kid on the block.

In high school I ran cross country for two years, junior and senior. My coach there was actually also the English teacher, Mr. Ward. High School teen boys are now taking a serious look at girls for the first time and I was no exception there. Mr. Ward had seen me in action with girls in his English class, so he certainly knew I had an interest in the opposite sex. Mr. Ward's training technique for cross country was to have you run up the municipal ski hill a couple times and walk down, then go for a two mile run if you had not already puked your lunch up. First day I did that routine I ran about a half mile till we got to some trees and I slipped into the trees and hid till the team was out of sight. I had decided girls were more fun than running, I guess, and went home. Next day I went to Mr. Ward to explain my lack of interest in cross country at that time. His comment was, "I know Steve, you're a lover, not a runner." In college I ran two years of cross country, again with average performance. I seemed to be a middle-of-the-pack sort of runner as a youth.

I took 10 years off from competitive running until age 28 or 29, when I saw a local race sponsored by the YMCA. I called the race director, Joe Ficcarro, and asked if I could come in with no training to see if I would like to run again. Sure enough, Joe said, "You're young and it's only two miles for the novice race. So I showed up in an old pair of tennis sneakers and finished almost dead last, behind two 12-year-old girls. I thought, *oh no, I can't be in that bad of shape at this age.* This would be the beginning of my more serious attempt at distance running. Over the next five to six years I worked my way up to marathons, and in fact ran a 3:02 at the 1977 Marine Corps Reserve Marathon in Washington D.C. Not world class by any means, but a top 10 percent finish is a good race by most standards.

So the stage is now set. I have running in my blood for a major portion of my life. Even in my senior years now I have taken up snow shoe racing and have qualified three times for the National Championships, with a best finish of fifth in age bracket. At the Empire State Winter Games I have several medals including gold at various sprint distances. I also won my age bracket at the Eastern Regional Warrior Dash at Wyndom Mountain. Not many after age sixty are crazy enough to try this one. It's an adventure race with military style obstacles and thousands of participants who seem to enjoy mud, water and fire for an afternoon outing. Beating a handful of sixty something athletes is a nice measuring stick of your condition, but having a faster time than some six thousand much younger people is a great example that you don't have to fear aging. Besides, it puts a really big grin on my face.

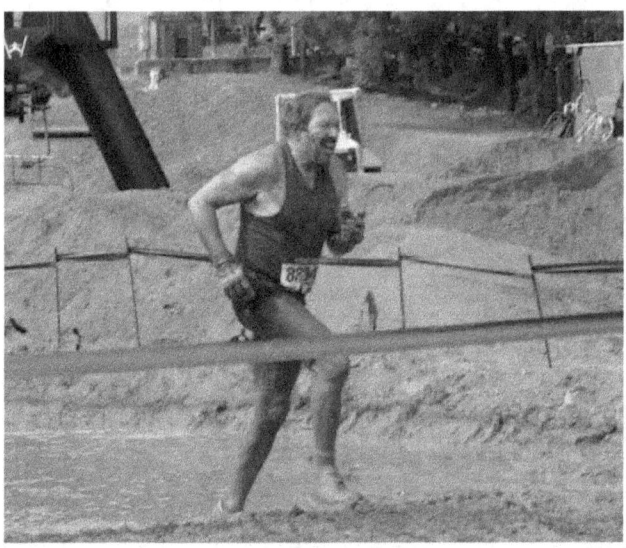

The warrior

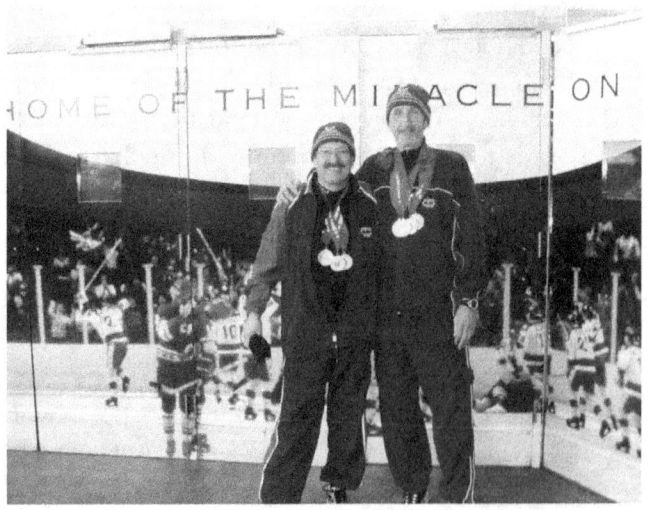

Steve with friend Kermit at Lake Placid

NUDE RUNNING

Now we can combine two activities all at once. Nude camping and running. Sound funny? It had been awhile since I was in a nude campground or been in a cross-country race and I somehow came up with the wacky idea that maybe you could do both at the same time. Don't ask me why, it just popped into my head. So I started to search the Internet to see if there was such a thing. Wow! What a surprise I got. There are lots of nude races all over the country. Shocked, are you? So was I. I'm thinking, I'm not the nut my wife thinks I am. I have been vindicated of radical thinking to be, at most, a little avant garde if not mainstream in the pursuit of the unusual.

Well, I found the perfect race and location. Just three and a half hours from home and slightly over the Canadian border at Niagara Falls was a nude family style campground that was having its annual Summer Fest. Summer Fest was really a marketing idea for the campground to let non- nudists come in on a clothing-optional day to see what the nude lifestyle was all about. The local chamber of commerce was involved and a 5K cross-country race was advertised to hopefully bring in some athletes. Like me, of course. In addition was a sports car show. If you were a car collector you could bring your ride and show off your pride and joy (your car body) as well as your own body and not have to have that silly sign that says, "Don't Touch Unless You're Naked." I knew my wife would not appreciate my going to anything resembling a nude festival by myself. I'm putting that mildly—she would likely lock me in a room and lose the key. What I needed was a male friend to go with me. I have to call my friend Ed, also an avid runner, but not a nudist by any means.

When I reached Ed I told him I wanted him to go to a cross country race with me that will be fun with lots of food and a car show. Ed is also a car enthusiast, so I knew that would create an added interest.

"Only one thing, my friend, we don't wear clothes for this race."

"What? Are you kidding me?"

"No, I'm serious."

He then tells me his wife would kill him if he went to an all-nude campground, race or no race. So I'm thinking, okay, let's invite both our wives and problem solved. Sure enough, the ladies said you two go and have fun. Understanding these wives are two of the most conservative ladies you could meet, I knew they would not go, so Ed and I got to have an adventure.

Once we arrived we were directed to park the car near an office for the campground and go in to register. Ed had no clue what the protocol was and looked to me for advice since he knew I had been to a nude campground before. I'm already taking off my clothes and throwing them in the car and he is looking at me like, "do I have to?"

"This is what we came for Ed. Drop those pants, man, and we will blend in with the crowd."

Now normally a naked person would stand out in a crowd, but here it is just the opposite—clothed people are the ones that draw attention.

After registration we went for a walk around the camp to get the lay of the land and see what all the activities were. The first cars I saw were twin sports cars driven by husband and wife. An Austin-Healy Sprite and an MG Midget. Basically they are the same car, so it's unusual to see a couple driving this British pair. A young couple, I would say in their early 30s, and both good looking to match the cars I'm sure. Oh no, I meant the nice looking cars match the owners. I'm not sure if they were club members, but I am sure they were buck naked and seemed to be enjoying themselves.

Continuing on our walk, we saw an outdoor pool, locations for games and activities galore. Since this was a fund raiser as well, the camp had offered various vendors of services or goods a deal to participate for free with the option to donate some profit to the camp. One such vendor was a massage therapist. Now I have been to a massage therapist before, so nothing uncommon there, but this is just a little different since the therapist is nude and so are the clients. There seemed to be a waiting list too. Gee, I wonder why. I would have to give it some thought. Actually, I was wondering if I had the nerve to try it out as a new experience. Obviously this would fall under the heading of scientific research. I was sure my wife would not want me to travel all this way and not have the full experience. Also part of the festivities was a real pig roast and there on a rotating spit was the whole pig basted and smoking a grand aroma throughout the camp. I was getting hungry already.

What we actually came for was a 5K nude race through the campground, so it quickly became running analysis time. Like, where does the course go and how difficult is the terrain? We found the camp race director and got a map and some directions since the run was largely through the woods on a trail that would take three loops past spectators in the open grassy areas and then the wooded trails again. It was not as rough as I imagined it would be, but it did have a couple challenging turns and a few bumpy places. Since you're going to run nude, we sure don't want to be falling down, now do we?

Ed and I do a little jogging to more or less test the theory that men can run without a jock and not pass out. Now I was pretty sure 3 miles worth of bouncing testicles would give you a headache at least. As it turned out, nature has its own protective way for us athletic-type men. During heavy aerobic exercise the scrotum shrinks and pulls those bouncy boys close to the body for safety. It's nothing short of amazing. On the other hand, if you're built so when you wear shorts your little boys fall out the leg hole, then don't try this at home.

Mind you Ed and I had run together for a long time, but this was a whole new experience for both of us and it turned out to be downright silly. I'm pretty sure Ed was not comfortable hanging with me nude because as I start to discuss our bouncing testicles and how funny this feels, he is not participating much in the conversation and informs me maybe we should just run our own race and forego pairing up for this event. By that time I was laughing my balls off, but then realize they may just fall off during the race. Our little test proved uneventful, so after one loop on the course we settled in to meet a few people and wait for our race to begin.

I did not see a lot of contestants around so I began to wonder how many would have the nerve to show up. Racetime showed me all nine runners including a healthy German girl complete with authentic accent and a strong full-figured body. After chatting with her for a bit I learned that she was staying just two hours away from this race and read about it in the local newspaper. She had been visiting relatives near Rochester and suddenly said to her husband and a close friend, grab your towels boys, were are going to a nude race. The husband and friend were not runners and would just hang around (no pun intended) while the race was underway. This would give Ed his break from running with me since I had this new-found friend to run with.

The campground has an indoor recreation area which includes a hot tub, toilets and showers. One shower in particular seems to be interesting as it apparently was made to shower more than one person at a time with its multiple shower heads and a glass door for water containment. Now I have seen outdoor showers at public beaches and swimming pools for rinsing, but this is a nudist camp and that brings a whole new dimension to a group shower that may not be gender specific. Later in the day I would discover just what implications that can have.

So race time comes up and it turns out there will only be about a dozen of us and the whole campground is going to watch us run three loops around the grounds. I have been on many race starting lines, but this one is surely different and I am trying to contain my giddy self as much as possible. I take a glance over at Ed and he has this look in his eye that tells it all. "What am I doing here" is written all over his face. I just may burst into laughter here at his expression as I hear the starter say go and off we run. I settle in next to "Miss Germany" and let Ed pull ahead.

Now I have his lily white butt fading into the distance and I'm okay with that because my peripheral vision is picking up bouncing breasts. It's only a small distraction, ha ha. Well, no, actually they were quite big and "Miss Germany" had a strong steady step. We seem to be finding a gap spot between the leaders and the back of the pack and settle into an easy pace. Conversational pace would be the correct term since that is just what we are starting to do—converse.

I soon learn that the nude life style is a job for this lady as she is a public relations person for a large nude beach and travels extensively promoting the nude life style. How about that for a job? My head is spinning with all kinds of questions on what it must be like to have a job like hers. In fact, the conversation is stimulating to the point that I have lost count of how many laps we have done. You wonder why running next to a full-figure nude woman would make you lose yourself. Thank goodness the club members are keeping track of the laps. Each time we went around we would come by the same members cheering us on and even though they are also nude, you do feel conspicuous bouncing around in front of a cheering crowd.

Upon completion, the activities director presents us with completion certificates for our efforts and we are now free to explore the party atmosphere of the day.

It was a warm summer day and we had worked up a good sweat, so a shower was in order. I'm looking for a shower in the recreation building and come on this glass door shower I had mentioned earlier, but it is in use. I stand waiting near the door to be next when I see that "Miss Germany" is the person in the shower. She sees me waiting and now explains this is a community shower, and to come on in because there's room for me, too.

When in Rome, do as the Romans do. So I jump in and take a shower right next to "Miss Germany." I figure no one would believe me at home unless I could show them the video, but alas you will have to take my word for it as there is no video.

Ed is still keeping his distance from me, especially now. We had been near the swimming pool and I overheard some women talking about the gay couple. You see they thought we were a gay couple and when I explained this to Ed, he directed me to go talk to some women and keep a distance from him. This was just too funny, so I figure he was really endorsing my showering with "Miss Germany" and that cleared any misgivings I may have had prior .

I had time after the race to consider another new experience while I was here at the campground: the massage therapist. Sure, why not? Time to broaden my horizons and do more scientific research. The line had gone down some by now so it was not too long a wait and after all, I did want to make my contribution to the fund raisers of the day. My therapist was a very attractive young lady and, yes, she was also totally nude. I laid on the table as directed and was trying to get relaxed to enjoy the massage. Imagine a nude woman running talented hands over your nude body, and just wait till you're face up. Truth is, you can get use to this and, no, I'm not going to answer that question on your mind. We make small talk, as I did have some curiosity about how she came to participate in the festival day, so I asked questions while thoroughly enjoying my massage. Did I mention this is an open air tent and people passing by can see you get your massage? It's a fact and just adds to the funky nature of this whole day. All in all, it was a great experience and even though it had an odd nature to it, this story has been told many times and gets eye-raising expressions every time.

I should mention there are a few hazards to this nude adventure. The sun and other natural elements can be harmful, so take a few precautions. Suntan lotion would be the obvious one. Certain parts of the human body that never see sunlight are especially sensitive, so lotion is important. Now putting it on in public can present a whole different issue. It's not quite the same as putting lotion on your nose when you go out to cut the grass at home.

Another caution would be having a towel to sit on for sanitary reasons, you just don't know who sat on that bench before you. I made the mistake once of going fishing in an aluminum canoe at a nude campground. Well, the mistake was not considering the aluminum seats were sitting in hot sun for an hour or two before I sat my bare bottom on it. Holy hot cakes, Batman, that seat gave me an instant tan. I would never go fly fishing in the nude either, unless you're a real pro you just may have to get help pulling that dry fly out of your butt.

Insect repellant is another good idea. Most of these nude campgrounds are in rural areas and have plenty of biting insects. One time I fell asleep near a pool and woke up to a stinging sensation. Swatting a deer fly off the end of your penis just doesn't look cool in public. That bite was one of the worst I ever had. Common sense applies here more than in most places, so take care if you decide to go bare.

How the Modeling Started

In my semi-retirement years, I found that my kitchen business had a few highs and lows. This gave me pause to wonder if a new income stream in the form of a part-time job could be beneficial, and give me "exposure" to new people in life (no pun intended). I have a close friend and neighbor that brought me a newspaper ad and pointed to it, saying, "Here is a great job for you Steve." The ad was from a local art institute looking for figure models, for drawing, painting and sculpture classes. Bob was familiar with some of my stories of adventure at nude campgrounds, and just figured it would be a natural fit. I don't think he really expected me to follow up on it immediately, however, I had the job the next day.

Apparently there is a shortage of male nude models in my town, and I stepped in at just the right moment. You may be wondering what the interview was like and if you have to audition. The answer is no audition. The biggest concern an art school may have is, will you show up on time for a class and if you can stand still for long periods of time. There isn't a big concern for your body shape either. All shapes are welcome, just stand still. The students are being taught how to draw the human body. They must learn how the details of all body shapes come together in order to study life and represent it in all forms.

I talked to my wife before I applied for the job, and as you might imagine, got quite a surprised look from her to say the least. "Are you nuts?" she asked. "You're going to stand in front of a class of young students totally naked?"

"Yes, dear, that is what the job calls for," I said. However, the students aren't always young. You never know who may decide to take an art class as a hobby, if not for a degree as well.

Bob and his wife, were very much interested in how my first day on the job would go, and frankly, so was my wife. Although my mother had been an artist and I had seen her paint as a teenager, she did outdoor scenes and still life, such as a bowl of fruit. So I really had no reference to life drawing, or just what I should do at the start of the class. It was a couple weeks before I got my first class, so I had plenty of time to back out. I became more apprehensive as the date drew near. I do remember that first day pretty well, even though it was several years ago. One good thing: you don't have to worry about what to wear for work, because you won't be wearing anything at all.

My first class at the arts institute was to start at 1 p.m. The class had been out to lunch, and students were slowly beginning to arrive, as I waited with great anticipation in the hall outside the studio drawing room. I had not met the teacher before, so I was just waiting for an older guy to show up. Some students saw me sitting nearby, and had that curious look on their faces, and that made me a little uncomfortable. Mind you it was my first nude class, and first time to model, so naturally I was a little nervous. This is not the same as going to a nature camp and having some casual conversations with other nude people. It was more like an auto mechanics class, with students leaning over an engine, while the teacher explains what makes this thing tick. In other words, a lot of close up scrutiny .

When the door opened to the classroom, I wandered in still looking for the teacher. I heard a young female student say, "Who is that old guy over there?" I looked over my shoulder for an old guy and realized she was talking about me. That didn't do much for my confidence. Soon the teacher walked in and immediately recognized me as the new guy on the block. I introduced myself to Greg, a good looking guy in his early 50s wearing a light blue shirt and jeans. I explain, that this is all new to me and ask if he can give me some help in how to get started. I knew nothing of what drawing lessons the students were getting, or what kind of a pose he would need from me, or how long I would have to hold that pose. Greg was really nice in pulling out a book that had male nude models in it, and suggested I look through the book to get some pose ideas. The drawings in this book were just incredible in their realism, so I took note of the artist that did them for future reference. The book turned out to be a biography on Paul Cadmus, an early 20th century artist, so check that out of your local library if you want to see some great figure drawing.

There are some really basic things one may never think of when doing a nude drawing session. Like where you get undressed, and where do you put your clothes? Seems simple enough, except this particular drawing room didn't seem to have a place for that. I ask Greg, and he points to a set of steel doors on the side of the room. This is actually a storage closet for supplies, and it is quite full. He tells me to go in there, get in my robe, and come out when ready. I'm thinking, the "when I'm ready" part may be quite a while, but of course I get started.

I close the closet doors behind me and undress, folding my clothes and placing them in a bag I had brought for just this purpose. I have a robe, slippers, and a towel, which are standard model accessories, as I had been instructed by the school. So now here I am all alone in a closet facing two steel doors with a class of about 15 waiting for me to appear. My heart is racing as I face the door and take a deep breath telling myself, *I can do this. Now, open the door and step out, Steve.* This was huge for me, as a first timer.

The room is not that large for the number of students, so I actually have to work my way through small openings between the students' easels to get on the model stand. Everyone is 360 degrees around the stand, so there is no real escape route, should I chicken out, and believe me, it crossed my mind. Greg is now explaining the lesson to the students, and I'm just waiting for instructions. He gives me the nod to remove my robe, and of course I'm thinking, this is the moment of truth. One deep breath again and off it comes. Oh, hey this isn't bad.

I'm just nude in front of 15 strangers, and suddenly wondering what they are thinking of this old man?

I have to tell you, the first time you drop the robe is a shocker. What do you do now? Well, picking a pose is the most important, so you better think of that before you drop the robe, because it's very awkward after if you're fumbling around with no direction. Your first thought may be to see how students are looking at you, and maybe get a read on what they are thinking. I can tell you, making eye contact is not something you want to do. It can make the student very uncomfortable, and certainly the same for you. So I look above or between or even at the floor, and try to pretend I'm alone after my shower. On your first day nothing really works, friends—count on it being awkward for you, and for any first time art students. The good news is the longer you do this, the easier it gets.

I'm thinking of a pose and hoping it doesn't look silly. As soon as I take one, I start thinking of what the next one will be. Let me see, did I just do that same pose a few minutes ago? The process repeats itself many times over in the average three hour class.

At my age, these students look so very young that I'm feeling like I could get arrested, but in reality they are 18 and up, and it's only me feeling kind of silly. The room is small enough that the model stand has but a few feet to the nearest students. This stand is 4 feet square, and about a foot tall. The elevation gives the student a better view of the model, and it gives the model the feeling of star status. I'm beginning to see how a performer on a theater stage may feel. Spot lighting is used to accent shadow lines, and this just enhances that theater stage feel. Realizing that these students are here to learn how to draw the human figure, it suddenly comes to mind, you're the most important person in the room next to the teacher. Certainly, on the first day this is not apparent, but as the years go by, I have come to realize I can actually have an impact on someone's education by creating interesting poses to motivate the student to want to do a better drawing.

On this day I am just plain scared, and more often than not, I am thinking of what stories I will be telling Bob and his wife and my own wife when I get home tonight. I know they are all waiting to hear about it. Mind you, most of my friends and my wife are very conservative people, and would never even dream of being seen nude, let alone in a room full of people staring at you. I'm thinking today, maybe I should be one of those conservative types, but I am determined to try this out and frankly, I think the rush of doing something this far out is driving me on.

One female student stands back from her easel, checks her drawing, looks at me, tosses her hair, adjusts her collar and seemingly is doing way too much primping for a drawing class. In my silly old mind I'm thinking gee, was that meant to tease me? Remember, I'm nude and flirtation of any kind is a no-no, especially in this environment. One's mind can play tricks and quickly I think how silly that would be considering my age. I do not make eye contact and continue to look past or beyond, but it is interesting how much your peripheral vision can pick up. Then, of course, I realize, that the room also has many young men her age, and all this primping is really for them and not the naked old man. Or is it? Hmmm.

Friday nights my wife and I usually play cards with Bob and his wife, so our first Friday after this class they were all anticipating hearing about my nude experience. I take my time, going step by step from the greeting with the receptionist to entering the drawing room. Their eyeballs are bugging out, and the grins on their faces are absolutely priceless. I think in reality, they are part of my reason for writing this book. I realized that although this may be routine for me today, it is certainly not for most people, and thus, I hope you are also finding it at least, a curious read. Smiles, amazement, laughter and head shaking abound, and I now have a captive audience for any future excursions into the world of figure drawing.

Greg had indicated his satisfaction with my performance in that first class, and said he would recommend that I be put on the call list for future classes. This gave me the idea to ask the receptionist who did the model schedule how many classes they actually had, and how many hours a month I might count on for employment. The answer was not as many as I had hoped for, especially if I was going to make this a decent-paying part-time job. I was thinking of more money, especially for doing a job that most people would never even consider. Actually, I thought they should give me hazardous duty pay, just like the Army did when they sent me to Vietnam. This wasn't the time to complain since it was my first day, so I hid my disappointment, and moved on to get home and tell my first day story. Soon though, I was inquiring around town as to what other schools offer art classes that might need models. My big surprise was that my own community college and alma mater had a great art department and they were actually looking for a new model.

I called the next day and left a message that was promptly returned by Jim, an art teacher who apparently did the hiring. Jim invited me to come in for an interview and show me their drawing studio, which I did within a couple days. Mind you, at the time I was about 62 years old, and was really wondering if they would accept a man of my age. As it turns out, age is not a factor in this work. They actually like people of different ages and body types, to make a broader life drawing experience for the students.

The interview seemed to go well and Jim introduced me to Jed, another art teacher sharing some of the same classes. The three of us went to see the drawing studio, which I found really interesting, being the newbie I was. The only time I saw these guys get a little concerned was when I asked about an erection. It occurred to me as a man, that in this working environment at some point in time it is possible to have that happen. Just a curious question on my part, I'm a curious guy. So I asked, what should I do if that happens? Should I stay where I am, or step down off the stand and excuse myself? Jim and Jed looked at each other with a hesitation and then Jim said, "Well, why would that happen?" That seemed odd to me, we all know why erections happen, it's that little brain thingy that goes off and sends blood to your penis.

That was not my answer, of course. I simply said, "I don't expect that to happen, but what if it does? The honest answer is that it rarely happens in a working environment. If it happened often, they would feel the model had the wrong motivation for this job. In all the years I have worked that is the most common question I get from men outside the art community. How do you take your clothes off in front of all those girls and not get aroused? It is a mindset of course. I'm here to show them how good their grandparents might look naked, and not to meet chicks.

Another question Jim asked was, "Would you be comfortable working with another model?"

This had never occurred to me before. "Male or female?"

"Either." This presented a whole new dimension to the job. Gee, I really like girls, but am I homophobic? No, but it did give me the thought of Ed back at the nude race and his not wanting to get too close to me. So my answer was, "No problem," but in reality I had no idea how that would go, so would just wait to see when it happens. Apparently I passed the first test, and I was invited to come back for a drawing session on another date, and subsequently invited to come for classes. This would happen within a week. Suddenly I was employed in two different schools as a nude model, and now presented with a new dilemma. Should I keep this a secret or not? After all, many people will think it strange, and I meet a lot of people in public, from my kitchen business to my sports activities. Two that I know of actually work at the college. And then there's the people at church, a lot of whom I've known most of my life.

THE CHURCH

Now this is getting interesting, to say the least. You see, I was the chairman of the board of trustees at my church. I figured I better jump in and tell them about my new job so it does not come back to them through some other avenue, and make it look like I was hiding something. Church people can be a little funny about you taking off your clothes in public. I'm thinking, *I am modeling for art, not stripping in a nightclub, so how hard could they take it.* Actually, I was pretty nervous. Conservative Christians in particular don't take well to being nude unless you're just taking a shower. Even then, I wonder if some don't do laundry and personal showering at the same time, by wearing their clothes in the shower.

When I get a little heat from religious people on nudity, I hit them with my version of Genesis at the beginning of the Bible. I explain that it was Satan who tempted Eve with the apple, and gave Adam and Eve knowledge that made them ashamed of their naked body. So a strong case in my mind, that clothes were the doing of the devil, and God actually made us nude. In fact, if God has made us in his own image, why would we be ashamed of that? Perhaps I over simplify here, but I love to confuse my friends on this issue. After telling my board members about my new job, I was surprised at how well they took it.

There was laughter and surprise, of course, but in general no one made a fuss or told me I should give up my board seat.

Ken, a young board member, asked me if I knew who worked at the community college as a model as well. This seemed to be a trick question because he *did* know, and it was a 19-year-old young lady who used to come to our church for vacation Bible school in the summer. She would also visit the church on occasion with her older sister, who was friends with a number of other teens who were members of the church, whom she knew in high school. Stephanie was her name, which by coincidence is also my daughter's name. I had first met Stephanie when she would have been about 12, when our church did vacation Bible school in a Renaissance theme. I was teaching archery as the Sheriff of the Shire, wearing green tights and looking very much like Robin Hood. I did not know her well then, as it was a passing experience in our craft sessions.

Our church had many teenagers who went to high school with Stephanie in later years and it was then that I had some general conversations with group teen meetings. Not close by any means, but we knew each other, and a few people in common were friends. Now let's get back to Ken. He is telling me that the girl I met at 12 was now 19 and a nude model at the same college. Suddenly I remember Jim who did my community college interview, asking me if I would be willing to work with another model. Wow, all of sudden that question has a whole new meaning, especially as I see Ken with a giddy smile on his face when he tells me this. I am sure other board members are thinking I must be off my rocker, but no one says so, at least not to my face.

STEPHANIE

From my experience, dual models are not common in the classroom. However, at this community college, they are an integral part of the learning experience, and I now believe other schools are missing the boat by not having them. I work solo at most places, but here I am often with another model, most often with a female. I have worked with men as well and in certain lesson plans that works quite well also. I'll have to admit, working with girls is a lot more fun. There is a totally different dynamic going on and I really think it motivates the students to a level of higher achievement.

Most often with two models we are on opposite sides of the studio, and the class gets divided in halves to work with one model at a time. That gives each student a chance to draw both in the same class period, which more quickly sharpens the skill level in proper rendering the gender differences. Also, larger classes can now get a closer view on the model, which is difficult with a single model. Class size can frequently be 18, and that is really hard to put around a single model.

Soon it was my first class at the community college and they had me working with Stephanie right off the bat. I was new to the job as it was, and just getting used to the nudity. Putting me with a female the first time was really pushing the learning curve, but I didn't tell anyone I was concerned.

It turns out Ken had had some contact with Stephanie, as they had been texting each other a bit. Unknown to me, Stephanie had a heads up on my coming to class and in fact had remembered me to some degree. I had not seen her in a while, but I did recognize her, as I came in early before class. There was a bit of a smile on her face as I approached, which seemed to tell me this was going to be a lot easier for her than me. After all, she was the more experienced model by far at that point. We exchanged a pleasant hello, nice to see you again, etc. I was full of questions about my new environment and I knew it was going to be a bit awkward.

"Stephanie, are you going to be okay with this?" I asked.

Her response was more to the point. "Steve, the bigger question is are *you* going to be okay with it?" Oh, she was so right about that. I find that young people today are often much more cavalier about nudity than my generation, but then, I'm not really one of my generation, mentally .

We would be sharing a dressing area that is very small. Literally about the size of two phone booths. We took turns using it separately, but the first thing I noticed was that we were both hanging our underwear in the open and in close proximity, which I don't even do at home with my wife. We get into our robes, and she explains a few house rules to set me at ease. Now it's class time, and this is the beginning of a semester, which means we are dealing with students most of whom have never seen a nude model before, as well as, this older man that had little model experience. Jim decides to have me watch and learn for a bit, and he puts Stephanie on a model stand in middle of the room with her robe still on. I move to the outside of the circle to observe.

Observation

On this day there is an anatomy lesson to start off. He explains to the class what they're going to be learning for the day, and the points to observe. Well, guess who else is going to observe? Stephanie is given the cue by Jim to drop the robe, and suddenly I'm saying to myself, "Oh my God, what am I doing here?" I'm also realizing how this must be for these young students because I'm generations older than they and been around the world. After all, I'm probably older than most of the students' grandparents. I'm still thinking *wow, that girl is really naked.* Well after all she is a pretty young lady with a nice figure and I am a man. Stephanie was right—it was going to be harder for me than for her.

In an anatomy lesson such as this, the teacher is up close to the model and pointing to features for the students to observe so they will know what to look for as they begin to draw. This means, you, the model, must be comfortable being a human example and be okay with having people up close and personal to scrutinize your every feature. Stephanie is a rock and unflinching through it all. She is a pro and knows what to expect and is very comfortable with herself in the nude. This would be the first of many lessons I would have to get used to and I have to say, it was Stephanie that helped me be at ease with the setting.

After this lesson the class was divided in half and Stephanie and I were placed on stands about 15 feet apart, but well within view of each other. I figure this must be like seeing her dad in the nude, but I have met her dad and know he is a bit younger than I. The class is three hours long so that's a bit of nudity for one day, but I would soon learn that we would do up to three classes in a row for a total of nine naked hours. It's really is a bit weird that you get to spend more time nude with a co-worker than most of us do with a spouse. This would be the first of many classes we would work together. I think we spent the better part of two school calendar years doing classes together.

We got so comfortable seeing each other that we could easily have a conversation about the weather, or anything else for that matter, while we were nude. Mind you, in between poses we both would robe up so we did not just stand around nude all day and chit chat. However, in the more advanced classes we sometimes did a pose on the same stand, usually imitating a classic fine art painting. The students are encouraged to create their own theme and not copy the original painting.

In this scenario Stephanie and I spent quite a few hours in very close proximity. This gave us the opportunity to whisper to each other periodically, which was a little risky because both of us have a sense of humor and would try to make the other smile or even laugh. On one occasion she was laying on her back with one leg bent up and one arm near her forehead feigning a death scene. I was seated on the platform next to her looking down on her. In the scene I am supposed to be mourning her death and be sorrowful in my expression. This is not easy. First of all, this is a nine-hour pose in three sessions of three hours each.

I'm looking down on Stephanie from the waist up as I am seated next to her hip. I have only a couple choices here—stare at her face or her breasts. You're not laughing are you? Gee whiz, what's a guy gonna do. Her eyes are closed, but she peeks now and then. We both agree we can't look each other in the eye for more than a few seconds or we will both burst out laughing. She whispers to me, "You don't look sad enough, remember I'm dead." It's all I can do to keep my composure, so I look off to her shoulder or her ear. Try this at home if you wish, sit nude next to a friend for three hours and let me know how that goes.

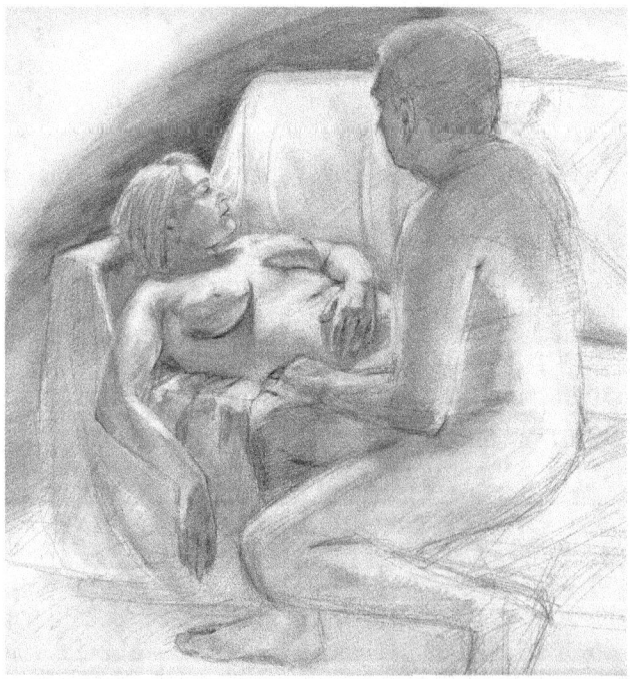

Death Scene

Poses with a story line or themes are favorites with both Jim and Jed when it gets close to the end of a semester. I think it's a great culmination of the lessons learned all term and the chance to showcase them in a single drawing. I felt like an actor playing a part in those scenes and we had a great time doing them.

I had been sharing this dual pose concept with an artist friend that ran a small art gallery. On Sunday nights she had drawing sessions open to the public in a room above their gallery. Anyone could walk in with their own equipment and draw for three hours for just a few dollars. Each week they would have a different model. Always nudes. After sharing my story of the dual poses Stephanie and I were doing she asked me if we would like to try that in a public forum. This would be a first because in our area no one had offered this to artists before. Stephanie agreed and we set a date. Now one thing I haven't mentioned yet about Stephanie is the fact that at the time she was a 3rd degree black belt in karate. Her karate form gave her many great poses and also provided a format for us to interact with our age difference and make it real.

The night we got to do our drawing session it was steaming hot in a second floor drawing room with no ventilation. It was a tight space with just enough room for a small model stand and maybe six artists at close proximity. They asked us to start with short action poses which was right up our alley. Stephanie would go on attack in a karate pose and I would take a defensive posture. One pose after another in short order would get us both sweaty as can be and we were nude so I can't imagine how the others felt. The results, however, were outstanding. I could hear exclamation of approval from a couple of the artists, so we continued on the same vain. This was a three-hour drawing session with an intermission about midway. At that point the director came over as we rested sitting on the model stand. Jan was her name, and she sat down next to us and spoke in a soft voice. "You guys are doing great," she said, "so good that the artists are already asking if you could come back again." We were both pleased as punch, and agreed that if we could find a mutual date we would be happy to come back. I must say it was a rare opportunity for both artist and model, and if you really like what you're doing it's a very satisfying experience. I might have called us the odd couple due to our age difference, but that did not seem to bother anyone there.

The amusing part of this night came after we were done. The neighborhood was not the best and it was well after dark, so I offered to walk Stephanie to her car. Halfway to her car I suddenly realize that she is the one with a black belt in karate, not me, and perhaps she should be walking me to my car. Fortunately, it was uneventful, and our night concluded on a happy but tired note.

The more hours you spend modeling the more drawings are made of you. That part did not occur to me early on in my modeling career. It probably did not occur to my wife either, but it did later. The artist has the say on what to do with drawings they have done of you, which basically means you are public domain. Suddenly you begin seeing yourself hanging on walls in class rooms and art display cases in student hallways and galleries. There were many pictures of Stephanie and I that were on display in a pose together. Now ask yourself, how would my spouse or significant other feel about that? As the years have gone by I have worked with about ten different women from 18 to 65 years old. There is a lot of art work out there somewhere with myself and other women in the nude. So you're thinking I'm either going to be a dead man real soon or my wife is a very understanding woman. Both could be true, but for now I'm living under the latter part.

In the beginning my wife sure didn't like the idea. When I first took the job she thought I was going to be alone in each session. Then she found out that there would be a female in the room too. The next stage was telling her that the girl and I would be on the same stand. Oh boy, I can still hear her comment on that "there isn't any touching is there?"

"No dear, of course not." In reality, however, there is some. On occasion we might be holding hands or be back-to- back. One time Stephanie and I were seated on a platform back-to-back with a pillow between us. The pillow kept slipping down and our backs would touch. I'm a typical Italian guy with a hairy back, which could be problematic in that situation. Stephanie would whisper over her shoulder, "God, you're itchy, move that pillow up." Now picture we are 45 years apart in age and having these conversations in the nude. That should give you an idea of how comfortable we were with both the nudity and the job. By the way, I have started shaving my back in recent years, not because anyone asked me to, but I just thought it would be better than me looking like a wooly mammoth in a drawing. There was another occasion where Stephanie and I would be more than close and totally push the boundaries for models that were not a couple or even looked like a couple. This was me, of course, trying to make an expression in art, and Stephanie willing to be a participant by making her own contribution. In reality, she was the art object with her curvy female shape, with me being the male strength supporting her.

I had an idea to do a black and white photograph with dark shadows or black background to accent our silhouetted shapes in an intermingling geometric display. This would be my first experiment with artistic photography. To do this I needed the assistance of a photographer friend who had a good camera and the semblance of a studio to control the lighting. Horace had a large clean garage, a professional grade Nikon, and he lived close by.

Prior to setting up a shooting date I looked up some contemporary classic art photography to get some ideas on what pose I wanted to try. The ones that really struck my eye required body contact. Here is where it gets a little dicey. First, I had to show Stephanie some suggested poses and get her approval. There was some hesitation, but she is a very game young lady and gets an A+ for courage from me. Next was getting approval from my wife on doing the photo at all. There was hesitation here also (no surprise there) but the idea was not completely shot down, so I proceeded with my plan. I know, you're thinking you would never let your spouse do that.

I had basically two ideas for the photograph. One was with our fronts facing each other and the other was back to back. Horace and I set up the makeshift studio the night before our shoot, including lighting and backdrop. Now this shot was my idea, but Horace was the expert on photography, so all the technology was his and the artistry was mine. He would suggest camera settings and I would frame the picture and set an auto timer so the shoot would be legitimately mine.

There were a couple other minor problems. One, Horace is a very conservative man and has never done any nude photography, so bringing a young female model into his garage was an eye opener. Second problem was needing a third set of hands to help Stephanie get into pose. That person would have to be Horace's wife, Sally, another ultra conservative who wanted no part of touching a nude woman or especially seeing me nude. Did I say these were minor problems? Fortunately, these people trusted me as an old friend, but I know their decision to help did not come easily.

In the back-to-back pose I would be leaning forward as in a running position. Stephanie would get a hand from Sally and climb up on my back with her butt nestled in the small of my back and we both reached back to grab hands over head to hold her in place. She had one foot pressed against my calf with her other leg raised and bent at the knee, with foot pointed ballet style. Our bodies were sprayed with baby oil and water to give light reflection, so we were pretty slippery, which was another reason Sally was there—for safety. When Horace asked Sally to come in I could sense some nervousness and her gaze was pretty much focused straight at the floor. Poor woman, I felt bad for what we were putting her through.

The second pose was front to front, and Stephanie had great reservations on this one because she was afraid of hurting me. We would attempt to make a letter "Y" shape, with me being the right side of the "Y" leaning back with legs firmly planted on the floor, while Stephanie would bend her knees and place them against my thighs. We then would hold each other near the elbows, while leaning backwards with heads pointed skyward. When explaining this pose to Stephanie, she looked at me like I was nuts. Since we were well oiled and slippery, she was afraid if her knee's slipped on my thighs she would knee me in the groin. In her words "Steve, if I slip I am going to kill you," and she would have, but lucky for us the whole thing worked out just fine, with the exception of making my friends very uncomfortable.

We would end up shooting over two hundred pictures to arrive at three I was happy with, and finally to the one I selected to frame. I still have it in my office. Undoubtedly, this will remain at the top of the most outrageous moments in the history of my model hall of fame. My wife Pat took a few days before she looked at the pictures, and had one comment, "Did you enjoy making those pictures, dear?" I have to give her an A+ plus for putting up with some of my screwy ideas.

STACY

Stacy was another young lady I had the pleasure of working with. This girl is a real-life "character" with a great sense of humor to match. She is more like one of the guys, and took no prisoners in the match of wits and sarcasm in conversation. She's a jock at heart, I think, but still a girl in every sense of the word. We had cycling as a common interest and when she told me she was moving and would no longer be in the area, I suggested we get one ride in together on my favorite bike trail. Stacy agreed, and we made arrangements to do a 10-mile ride along a canal route on the north side of town.

We could talk as I might with one of the guys, and ride side-by-side most of the time, as there was little traffic on the trail that day. After a while, Stacy seemed very uncomfortable on her bike seat and asked to stop for a minute.

"Wait," she said, "I have to make an adjustment," as she reached into her shorts to remove a piece of jewelry that was adorning her private area. If she were a guy it might be the customary testicle adjustment when riding trails for any distance, but this was different for sure and she had no embarrassment whatsoever. I just smiled with a chuckle, because this was typical Stacy.

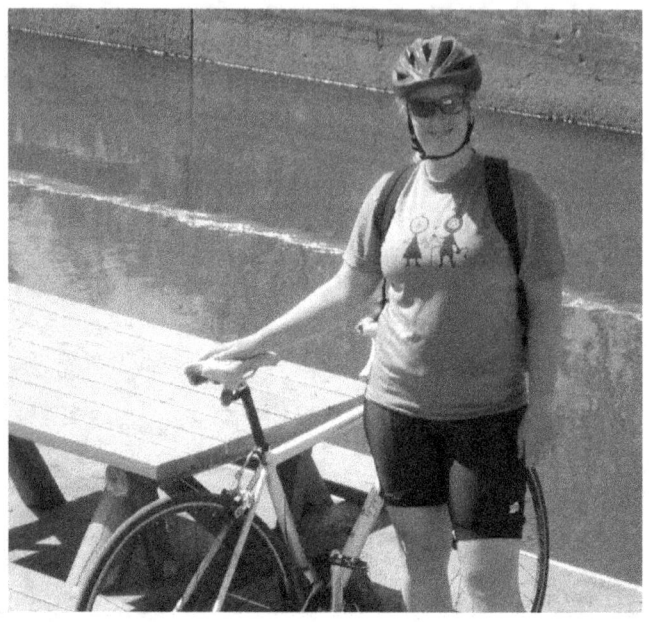

Stacy with her bike

When we had first met and started working the same classes, I had a feeling she was a little different. That thought was confirmed when we got talking about her tattoo one day. You see, she had a tattoo where no one would normally see it, unless you were really intimate. However, since we work in the nude, it was visible to me. Not that I was looking mind you, but it was across the top of her private area and in text. The text was too small for me to read without really staring, or at least being in close proximity. Not something I was going to do, friends, but I'm not beyond asking either. "Stacy, I don't want to stare at the tattoo, so maybe you could tell me what it says?" Obviously intended for a close-up read, it says, "lucky you." You may not see the humor, but I could not look her in the eye without laughing after that.

One day after working a class together we retired to our dressing area, taking turns using it to get dressed. This time I let Stacy go first, mostly because the area is so darn small. Neither of us have any shyness, so we could actually have dressed together, but that would be like you and your spouse going in your closet to get dressed. Some of you perhaps do that just for fun, but hey, this is a co-worker and not my spouse. Stacy comes out and waves goodbye, leaving me the dressing area. I go in and start to organize what might look like my laundry pile at home, so I can get dressed. After a minute I realize my underpants are missing. So, I'm looking high and low under shelves and on the hooks, under my coat and shirt, etc. and no undies. Now I'm thinking, *oh no, it's a Stacy practical joke and she took them.* I yell to Jim the teacher who is still in the studio. "Jim, I think Stacy took my underwear." He is laughing as I explain I can't find them, and then he tells me there is no way he is going to come in to help me look. Funny man.

Stacy is long gone by now and I'm faced with going home without my shorts and perhaps having to explain how that could be, if my wife sees me get undressed at home. Oh sure, this is going to fly real well. I didn't want to accuse Stacy of taking the undies. Did she hide them as a joke? Maybe she had an underwear fetish. Finally, I decide to text her and ask if she took them.

"No way man, I wouldn't do that."

The underwear had been missing for several days when suddenly they appear, all nice and laundered. Stacy now has to admit that she found them in her bag, apparently along with a sweater that must have been hanging over them on a hook. I was not going to let her off that easy, so Jim and I had to tease her about her underwear fetish for several days. Just as with Stephanie, we had several poses together in close proximity where we enacted a scene while looking at each other for a three-hour class. I have to say in this working situation it really helps if you have a good rapport with the other model or it can be really awkward. We did just fine and I was glad to make her acquaintance. I know you may be laughing at my description of making someone's "acquaintance" while working in the nude. It does bring a whole new meaning to the term "workplace."

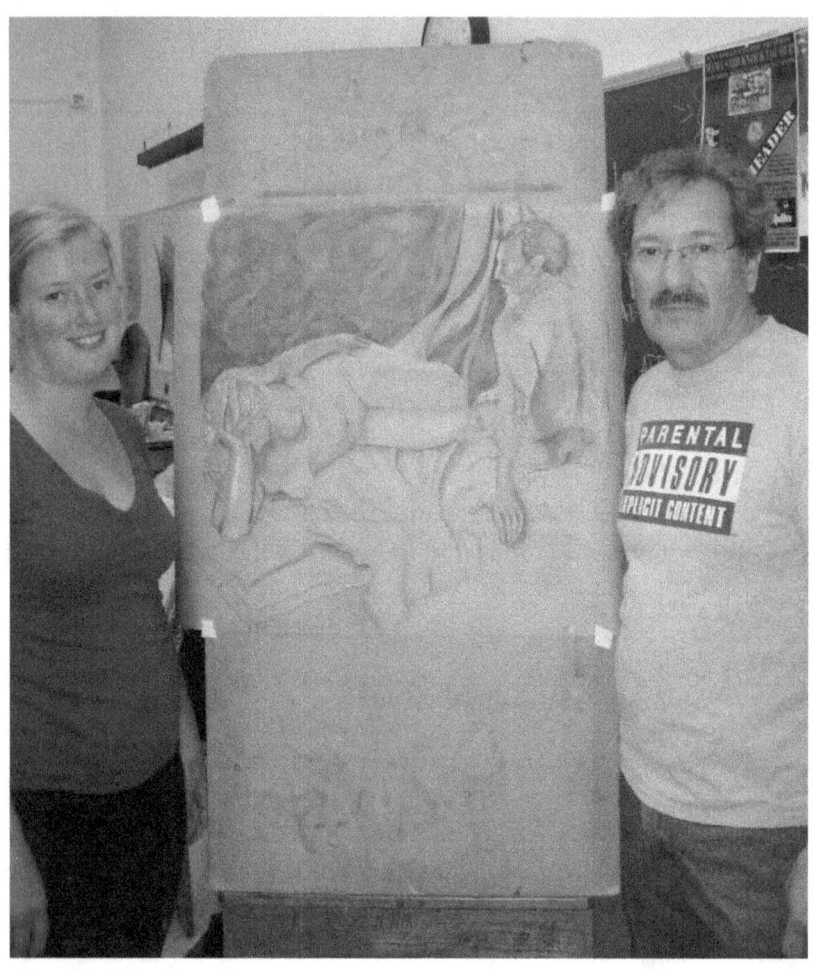

Stacy and Steve

IT TAKES ALL TYPES

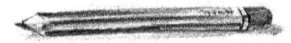

You have now heard me talk about two young female models. However, they aren't all young and they aren't all females, either. One of my favorite stories is of a gal named Betty. In the early part of my working as a model I figured I should keep up physically, for a couple of reasons. One is just plain vanity. The first drawings I saw of me had this really round belly that I thought I didn't deserve. After all, I used to be a runner. "Used to be" is the operative phrase here. Second, and more important, is the fact that the job is actually very physically demanding. Try standing with your weight on one leg, while having a body twist, for 20 minutes, and repeat this pose for three hours. Here is where I decided to get back to the gym and lose a few pounds.

It was at my local senior center that I met Betty. She and her husband had moved back to town after having been away for many years. Retirement and wanting to be near some old friends and family brought them back. Most of my friends at the center knew I was a model, so it was no big deal to discuss my job from time to time. Betty, overhearing my conversation one day, asked a few questions and was floored by the thought I would do such a job. She was obviously a modest woman and thought it was nuts. She told me personally one day that she would never do such a thing. I realize it's not something most people would do, but geez, cut me a little slack here.

I would go to the gym at least three days a week and often would ride my bike there, or jog and do a workout after. About two or three months into this program, I see Betty working out like crazy, and noticed she had also lost some weight. Just kidding with her I said, "Hey, Betty, you're looking great, are you thinking of coming to work with me at the college?"

I thought I would get a chuckle at least, but instead I got a serious, "Yes, I think I will." I'm not really believing this. This gal is way too conservative. She did say it very seriously, but that little smile with it just did not convince me. Sure enough, about two weeks later, she showed up at the college and got the job. Jim the teacher had given me a heads up a couple days before, so it wasn't a complete shock to me, but certainly a surprise. What changed her mind? This was going to be interesting to say the least.

The whole weirdness factor comes back in play just as it did with Stephanie, but in a different way. Betty was about 65 and married, not 19. Plus, I also knew her husband from the gym. It wasn't long before Betty and I were on the same model stand, looking at each other face to face just a foot apart. Now I'm thinking, *How am I going to look your husband in the eye at the gym next time.* After our first class of being on the same stand, I told Betty I thought she handled that really well, but that is exactly what she was going to say to me. Definitely on the strange side the first couple classes, but we got used to the situation soon and became good friends. I asked her husband one day how he was with her doing the job and he had little concern, just saying she was a big girl and could do as she wished. Let's face it, spouses often are jealous, especially when young, but as we age I think the confidence factor in our relationships relaxes those feelings. I know in my own case that is true.

Now the bigger question here is, why did Betty change her mind and decide she wanted to try this new adventure out? It was that old thing called "stepping out of the box." Betty had a successful business of her own and so did Jim, her husband. Perhaps she was not prepared with something to do in retirement. In her own words to me, "I was looking for something new to do and just felt like stepping outside the box." There is no doubt that if I had not brought up my model job at the gym, she never would have thought about it. So, I'm smiling because I made a difference in someone's life. I'm confident it was a good difference because I know Betty enjoyed modeling. There is, however, a sad part to the story. Betty's husband Jim had a stroke that left him impaired on one side. They had a two- story house that made it really difficult for him, so they moved back south where they also owned a one-level home.

Kayla

Kayla was another female model working later in life. When we first met I think she was in her early 50s and she was a much more experienced model than I. She had a bachelor's degree in Fine Art and was an accomplished artist herself. This gave her a double advantage with both experience and knowledge of the subject. I just loved her poses after she finally got into them, but it was so amusing to watch her wiggle this way and that, and then do it again, till she got the ants out of her pants. Oh, no pants. In reality it wasn't but a couple minutes, it just seemed longer. Kayla was a perfectionist and just wanted to get it right. She has my admiration.

Kayla was the second model I worked in dual pose with and we did many of them together including Adam and Eve (how appropriate). Perhaps the teacher chose Adam and Eve because we were the oldest model couple .

She was a bit of a health nut, always having one of those drinks that is full of natural things that make it like a full meal in a bottle, but looking like a sample from the local sewage plant before purification. Yet she had as many colds as anyone, so I passed on the drink offer even though the ingredients came from her own garden.

I "fell" for Kayla one night, really hard. We were both attending a performance in the theater at the college with her being seated in the front row, and during a break I wanted to go down to say hello. I tripped on the way down and hit my head on a railing. Everyone gasped as I lay prostrate on my back and starring at the ceiling, wondering what happened. My wife, who was still up above, had absolute panic on her face when she finally reached me. So much so that I felt bad for her. I was fine, but here comes Kayla thinking I am injured and offering to give me a ride home because I should not drive after such a fall. What a sweetheart.

Not Always Women

It doesn't happen too often but I do get to work with a few men. I have to say girls are a lot more fun, but then you might expect me to say that, now wouldn't you? What we have to look at here is the dynamic of the artwork we are going to produce. Does it make a good lesson plan for the student and will it make a nice portfolio piece? In a dual pose there is usually interaction between the models. Each model may be different in their approach to posing for a drawing, so putting two models together can be an interesting task and I am sure a few professors have dreaded the possible outcome. Enter my model friend Mike. Mike and I are both in our 60s and in pretty good shape, which allows us to do some pretty physical action poses. He is about 5' 8" and 180 lbs with grey hair on his head and no hair anywhere else. Yes, I said none. I, on the other hand have dark hair and enough for both of us on my body. If they ever recast King Kong I may apply.

Action poses are my favorite and I will commonly do super heroes or sports action like running, archery, baseball or tennis. This is where my experience in running races and other sports activities comes in handy. I may use props for these like a baseball bat or tennis racket. It is important to consider how long the pose will be before you take it. You don't want to be over reaching or leaning off balance if you have to stand for long periods of time. Trust me, you will fall over. This is where Mike excels.

I have never seen another model so energetic at any age, let alone over 60. I am convinced Mike is part monkey with his ability to take almost tree hanging poses and hold them for extended periods. The first time I saw him pose I came to the class to draw as well as to observe another model, which is a rare opportunity and can be a great learning experience as well. Mike is on a stand with a wall behind him and students are at stations in a semi-circle facing him. I am off to one side toward the back so I have a great observation point.

Suddenly he lurches, projecting one leg forward off the stand out on to a box a foot away yelling a scary, "aaaaahhhhh" sound while holding a spear-like stick in one hand thrusting it almost over the head of a young lady directly in front of him. Remember, this is a 60-plus naked man we are talking about. The girl just about jumps out of her seat with her head ducking in one direction and a frightful look on her face that was so priceless I wish I had a camera ready. I, on the other hand, have all I can do to keep some composure or I am going to lose it bursting with laughter. I really did not imagine an art pose that would get you out of your seat. I hear a murmur of reaction from other students as well and I can see facial expressions all over the place with a mix of shock, giddy smiles and "Oh my God I better draw this fast." Once the initial shock wears off one realizes this is a great action pose and you wonder how long can Mike stay in this position. It turns out it's a lot longer that you might think and this is where he shines.

One pose after another in dramatic fashion, up close and personal to say the least. You could say it was more of an exercise video in dynamic tension, or you could also realize the students are drawing like crazy because they also know this is a rare model opportunity and now is the time to take advantage of it. In the words of the famous Greek philosopher Horace, "Carpe diem" or "seize the day." One pose after another Mike lurches here and there like the monkey I think he is, elevating and swinging as if in a South American rain forest flying from tree to tree. Now freezing like an early cave man searching for his next meal.

Mike has done some performance art on request in New York City. Performance art basically turns a model into a live art display. On one occasion the gallery owner was storytelling in various art forms. The story was of a Japanese man that had been arrested for a murder in France in 1981. Issei Sagawa of Japan was studying at the Sorbonne

Academy in Paris when he lured a fellow student to his apartment on false pretenses and murdered her. The Dutch female student Renee Hartevelt was his selected victim because of her good health.

Sagawa had been small and sickly as a child and apparently grew up with the demented view that eating a healthy human would be of benefit to his own health. In fact, after shooting her in the neck with a rifle, he first attempted to eat her buttocks by biting into them, but with no success. He then went to a butcher shop and bought a knife to carve up pieces of her to be eaten later. When trying to dispose of the body by dumping it into a river he was seen and subsequently arrested.

His wealthy father hired an expensive lawyer who drew things out to the point that the French court had him declared insane and unfit to stand trial. Meanwhile both in France and back in Japan this bizarre story was making Sagawa a lesser celebrity, to the annoyance of the French, who really just wanted to be rid of him. The resolution to this problem was extradition to Japan, and let them worry about him. Interestingly, the Japanese found him sane and since the French refused to share any criminal details on the then-secret case, he was released and remained a free man.

Mike's gallery owner acquaintance asked him to model for a performance art depiction of the Sagawa story, live in his gallery. Now we have a brave model in Mike, totally nude on display for walk-in art enthusiasts to see what many thought was a wax figure, with the phrase "eat me" written on his chest in red. In his own words Mike revealed to me how he would stand so very still that patrons got the idea he was a wax figure, and would actually touch his wrist in a reality test, which gave him the opportunity to scare some folks by blurting out a grunt and moving. Here is a man with a sense of humor not to mention a taste for the bizarre. My hat is off in salute to his independent nature.

Back in our college class one day Mike and I were doing some dual poses that required some depiction of a story line and I am thinking, yikes, two naked older men, what is this going to look like? We've done a tug-o-war by using a big rope with each on an end, straining muscles or so it seems, trying to make it look hard without getting fatigued. On one occasion I introduced a Spanish dueling sword as a prop. Mike would lay on his back with me standing over him, with sword in hand, I make it look like I am stabbing him in the side.

Always thinking of what pose we will do next so we can keep continuity, I have these ideas popping in and out of my head. I'm also conscious of keeping it fluid with symmetry that makes a good drawing and being careful to be non-sexual in content. Let's face it, we are not doing nude mud wrestling in an art class. The next pose would be pushing the boundary on that subject. I hand Mike the sword and suggest he attack me from behind, as in, perhaps taking me prisoner. My description to him is brief and I am letting him more or less finish my conceptual thought, which could be risky if you're both not on the same page.

I am trusting in that we are both very comfortable in the nude and secure in who we are as individuals. Well, I tested that statement to the limit when Mike reaches around the front of my neck with the sword taken more like a knife to my throat, requiring him to be very close behind me and I am checking out the facial expression of a young female student directly in front of me and only a few feet away. What I am seeing is absolutely priceless as she looks me right in the eye with a little smile that seems to be asking me, "Are you okay with this pose?" She doesn't waste any time diving into drawing this, knowing it's likely to be a one-time pose. Later, she said, "That was an interesting pose." Apparently she didn't have a problem with the proximity of our bodies and I am happy to hear we didn't scare anyone. I look forward to the next time working with Mike.

STINKY FEET

Working in the nude presents interesting situations that you may never think of in your standard nine-to-five job. Normally when you get up in the morning to prepare for a day at the office, you most likely would lay out some clothes, perhaps checking them for pet hair and unsightly stains, and give the shirt or blouse arm pits a quick smell test. Let's take a quick shower after breakfast, make sure to brush the teeth and put on some deodorant before dressing. A check in the mirror tells you all is right in the world as long as you are presentable. Now, if I had a factory or blue-collar job, perhaps I wouldn't be so fussy knowing I was surely going to get those clothes dirty today. Plus, a manufacturing job is most likely to have some chemical smells with it and higher sweaty temperatures, making deodorant a much less important issue.

Now, let's take a look at my model job and make a few comparisons. First and foremost, I only need the clothes to get by security, because once inside the drawing room, I'm going to get naked. My consideration for daily pick of wardrobe is more likely to be how easy it is to take off and put on, because I won't be wearing it very long at all. While I am actually in work mode, those clothes are nowhere to be seen. This makes a whole new case for how clean the body is before you get dressed to drive to work. Now that arm pit smell is much more important. God forbid you should have a diarrhea attack just before leaving the house or even worse, as soon as you get to the studio. This is not an odor you want to advertise and, remember, students can be just a few feet away so if I see a nose wrinkle I know I am in trouble. Perhaps you're a female and you just started your period. That is not a naked experience anyone wants to have or witness. Now, we are taking a reality check on just how important personal hygiene is .

Knowing the potential for embarrassing moments is key to this job and I will go to great lengths to prevent the next day's college newspaper headline from reading, "Steve farts on model stand." Well, that is problematic, to begin with. You see, I do a lot of bending over, which is hazardous on a good day, let alone a gassy one. Try to get that picture out of your head. You see I use a timer set for the pose length, which I set at my feet. So I have to bend over to turn it off when it rings. Those who may sit behind me will often see me crack a smile, which in this case is not a good thing. Yes I am being silly here, but I do take the job seriously, so I do my best in the hygiene department. Consider also that I often work with another model and we may be in close proximity for an extended length of time, breathing the same air .

This brings me to another moment in my model history, that shall live "in infamy." Toward the end of one semester my instructor Jed had planned a series of theme drawings and came up with an Adam and Eve scenario in order to have a male and female in the same drawing. A young Eve would be played by Anna, whom I had met just a couple times previously as we had worked a few classes together, but always on opposite sides of the studio. We would be sharing the same dressing area separately as I had mentioned before with the Tracy story. I am a ladies first kind of guy, so I offered the area to Anna. When it was my turn I just about gagged on some kind of stink that I could not identify. Holy crap, was there a dead mouse in there? Or perhaps Anna had a moldy piece of limburger cheese in her lunch bag. Time and time again I would always find that odor in this tiny little space that had no outside ventilation.

When it came time for the pose Jed had selected, I would be kneeling at Anna's feet looking up at her as she looked down at me while handing me an apple to fit our scene. It was at this precise moment I began to realize where that smell was coming from. It was Anna's feet. I can tell you as an athlete having been in many men's locker rooms that this was the worst foot odor I have ever come across. Certainly this pretty young lady could not be the cause of the odorous catastrophe I was experiencing.

Now I realized the waft of bad air in the dressing area came from a pair of rubber Crocs that Anna wore daily and apparently never washed. When in pose I looked down and noticed the not only smelly but very dirty feet. These looked like the feet of "shoeless" Joe Jackson after a baseball game on a rainy day. Each time our pose broke I would move away to get some fresh air, knowing that the break was brief and I would have to return to my now practiced short breathing exercise so I wouldn't end up turning blue in an ambulance while waiting for the respirator.

Being a co-worker, it was not my place to bring Anna's attention to the problem. I felt bad, but this was not a situation to be tolerated without a gas mask. I was recalling my Army basic training literally in a gas chamber with a drill sergeant making you take off your mask with a room full of tear gas to repeat your name rank and serial number till you choked enough to understand how important the gas mask is and how to put it on in an emergency.

Jed was getting the sense something was wrong and was whiffing the air and looking at me. I had to tell him it was Anna, which he had a hard time believing. After several smell tests he finally agreed, and the issue of how to tell her followed. One suggestion was just to leave a bar of soap next to her Crocs. You had to think she would know, but somehow it did not seem to be a problem for her. This was not just my complaint, but several students also noted as the room itself became permeated with the smell of that large block of invisible moldy Limburger. No one seemed to have the courage to tell her and it seemed like forever when about a week later she was told in a private office meeting by two instructors that there was an issue. It wasn't much longer and the semester was over and Anna was moving out of the area, so problem solved. Some people just have stinky feet due to some chemical imbalance I guess. Suffice to say that hygiene in this job is critical.

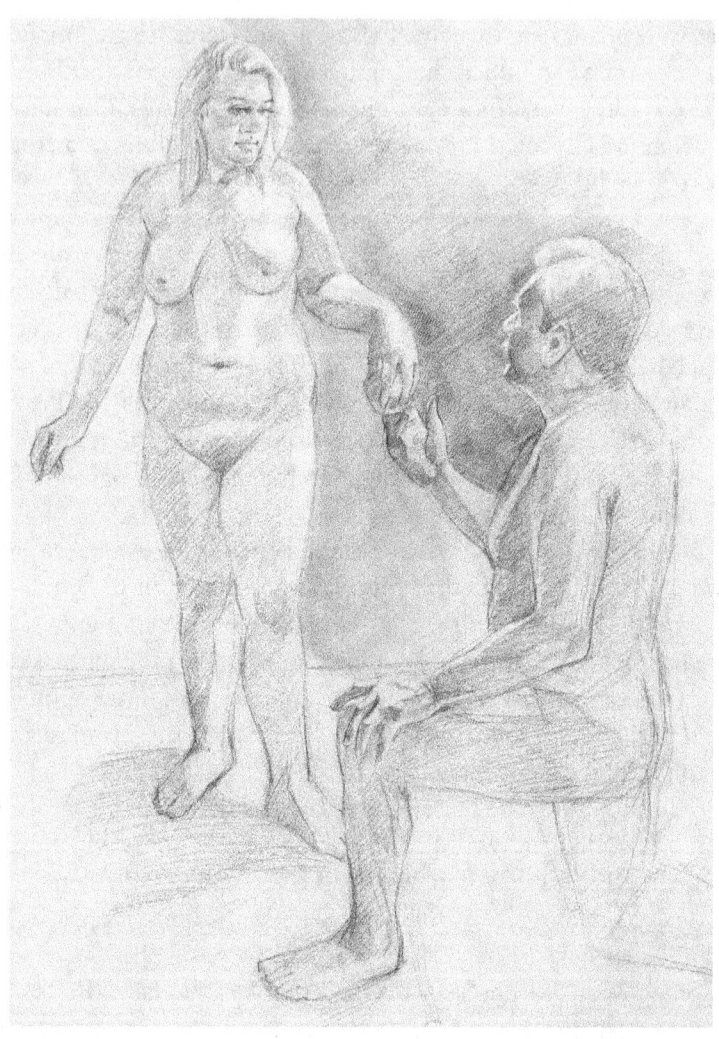

Stinky Feet

DEVAN

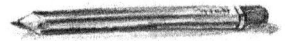

I have been fortunate to make the acquaintance of many art students who really enjoy what they are doing and it shows in their presentation. Realize that most of their artwork that I get to see is of me. How much "me" can a person take if not a true narcissist? Let me get back to you on that, right now that Bogart line "Here's looking at you, kid" comes to mind.

Devan is an attractive young redhead with fair complexion, freckles, a great big smile and curvy shape. A student of art doing a great job. I knew I was going to like her the first day we met. She walked right up to me and stuck her hand out saying, "Hi, I'm Devan, it's nice to meet you." It was the first time a student approached me knowing I was the model and introduced themselves with such confidence.

It was some time later in her second semester that she came to me asking about becoming a model, which surprised me since the average art student I meet is 18 to 22, and imagining them posing nude seems a stretch for me. Many art schools do not allow a current student to model, so with this in mind I gave Devan tips on other schools in the area where she could model. You might ask, what brings a young lady to want to model in the first place?

In Devan's case, it was something new to try, and she would gain confidence in herself as a young woman. It's certainly a big risk for almost anyone to put themselves on the line like this. Gee whiz, let's take off our clothes and stand nude in front of a group of strangers and see what they think of my body. For most people this is like climbing into a barrel to go over Niagara Falls and wondering if the barrel will hold together. The barrel held together just fine for Devan and she has gained a great deal of confidence in her own skin.

The first class she worked happened to be the same art institute that I had my first class in and she undressed in the same little paint closet where I stood frozen in anticipation on my first day. It was a funny coincidence, so we compared notes on this first day stuff and it was pretty funny how similar it was for both of us. She also realized the room was the same room she took art classes in as a young teen when her mom was teaching at the institute.

Devan was a little nervous of course, but she wasn't completely a neophyte here. Her mother had been an artist and art teacher so she did have exposure to nude art before. In addition, as an art student she certainly became familiar with my modeling and a couple of others from her classes.

Even with those connections to nude art there is still something uniquely terrifying about taking your clothes off in front of a group of strangers. When asking Devan how she approached this dilemma, I got a surprise answer. She imagined she was dressed the whole time. Don't look down and certainly don't look in a mirror, was her advice. It worked for her, greatly reducing the fear of public nudity and off she went to stardom. I say stardom because the teachers that have seen her model all say they love her natural way to fall into a pose with grace and confidence.

Stardom wasn't quite that easily achieved, however. There are always obstacles in any advancing career. First there was a boyfriend in the picture and I can tell you from my conversations with other models this can be problematic. The boys just don't like the fact that others are seeing their gal nude and especially because the students get to take home the drawings. Devan actually took the job without the boyfriend's knowledge and it was some time before she told him about it. When she finally did break it too him there was resistance, but it wasn't too long before he got used to the idea. Hurdle number one was out of the way.

This section is for women only. Men take a pause here and come back in a couple paragraphs. The dreaded monthly cycle is bad enough for women in the workplace, but imagine the nude workplace. Oh yeah, sounds impossible, but we have to deal with reality here. This is life as it happens. Usually a woman would plan ahead for this and it's certainly permissible to wear underpants for this occasion. No instructor would refuse this request. However, these things aren't always on time now, are they ladies!

As bad luck would have it, Devan was in a class as a model when her period showed up a full week early. She was not prepared for this and sought the help of the instructor who, thank God, was a woman. Imagine having to go to your male instructor with that situation. Also keep in mind that this is a co-ed class, so we are trying to keep the guys out of the loop here. Instructor Lynn is very cool as she goes to each female student one at a time and privately looks for some sanitary help. Finally one young lady has what is needed and Devan is able to finish her class without missing a beat and none of the guys were even aware of the circumstance.

Teachers will sometimes need to pose a model in situations that might stretch your imagination on how the final drawing is going to look. This may employ the use of props or furniture to get the desired look. In one situation, Devan was asked to climb up on a box that was seated on the model stand. Not a problem with a short box, but if you use a tall box to go for more height we just might be getting risky. Sure enough, as Devan attempted to climb on top of the tall box she lost her balance and tumbled down. Not high enough to really get hurt mind you, but remember she is totally naked and comes tumbling down sprawling limbs in all directions. This is the equivalent of the ever-graceful flying squirrel missing a jump from tree to tree. The teacher is aghast and runs to her aid, but this is a male teacher and he is decidedly fumbling to not pick up a nude female model. No problem, Devan is fine and back on her feet even as the class is making oohs and ahhs, asking if she is okay.

Falling asleep during a pose can be an occupational hazard on some days. I have done this myself a few times. You can get relaxed in a comfortable pose with the aid of some music playing and the right room temperature, off you go to snoozy land. This is particularly dangerous for a male model since we may dream of something sexy in our sleep which of course leads to an erection.

On one occasion, Devan was on a break with the class out of the room. She took the opportunity for a little nap laying down on the model stand. When the class returned the teacher had observed her sleeping and decided this would be a good pose to draw. He woke her up and told her she could just remove her robe and stay as she was. The rest of the class was spent on this pose and Devan had an easy day of it.

Suffice it to say, stardom in modeling does not come without a price and Devan was learning all that comes with the job in a short period of time. She has since modeled for non-instructional artist groups and gotten good reviews there as well. On the unusual side of things, I reversed the table on her and came to one of her model sessions to draw. I did ask her if she would be okay with that since I had been her model for some time this could be really weird. In fact, I had modeled for this same group of artists myself on occasion so this would be different for me as well. Devan said "Sure, let's give it a shot" and I did attend.

It was really strange at first for both of us, since our roles were reversed. In Devan's case there was some concern her mentor was observing and she wanted to get it right, I think. In my case, I was used to seeing her dressed and drawing me nude several times a week, so this was just a little on the nutty side. We both smiled and laughed at the awkwardness for a bit, but soon we were sharing at the breaks on how good her modeling was and how bad my drawing is. Did I mention I was 68 and she was 18?

APRIL

Most of the female models I have worked with have been either younger or older, but not many in the middle. Younger for me would be anyone under 50, but in this case I mean under 25 and older would be 55 plus. When I met April, she was about 32, with three kids and a husband. Not your common picture of a nude model. Even I was quite surprised at the married-with-kids place in life. Betty was the only other married gal I had worked with, but she was almost my age and in a very different place in life than April. Having three boys with school activities makes for a busy schedule by itself, but try adding two part time jobs to that and it seems like just plain chaos to me. A family life that also included church with its own event calendar would make it seemingly impossible and yet April did it all.

I know I painted a picture here that is making people scratch their head and wonder how April came to be a nude model or even why she would as a mom. It's really very simple: It's a job that paid better than average wages and it fit with other part time jobs and the school calendar. When she consulted her husband on the possibility, he was very supportive. He said, "If you have the confidence to put yourself out there, then go for it."

You would never guess April had three children. I can attest to this since we have worked together often. Another feather in her cap. I have to say it was a little strange for me to be in a scene with her, knowing there was a family at home and I was working naked with their mom and wife.

Speaking of wives, my wife Pat rarely got to meet the models I worked with, which maybe is a good thing. Sometimes I think I might be pushing the envelope on her tolerance for my job. We have often met students in public places where I usually got big smiles, waves and even a hug on occasion. Pat's comment was always, "Another student, dear?" But one night we were getting out of a movie late and April was working at the theater. She came right over to say hi to me with her usual friendly smile and I introduced her to Pat. After a short conversation on the enjoyment of our movie, we started out of the theater and Pat said, "I suppose she is another student." Now I was smiling as I said, "No dear, April is another model and I work with her." I thought it was amusing, but Pat turned around to check out April one more time and said, "You work with her?"

"Just part of the job dear, just another naked lady." Somehow I don't think she was amused.

NOT ALWAYS NUDE

When you think of figure modeling you naturally think of nudes, but drawing classes also study portraits and costumed figures. You may be surprised to hear some of my favorite moments in a studio have actually been dressed. Costumes give me the opportunity to get into some interesting characters and be an actor, if you will. They also add color and storytelling backgrounds. Add staging with lights and I'm elevated to superstar status once again. Now, I could be Robin Hood, King Arthur, a cowboy, or a spy with an eye patch. David, an instructor at the art institute, had a flair for the dramatic, a witty if not dry sense of humor and a penchant for illustrating hero type characters. So much so that he even played matching theme music to fit the costume and amuse the students. Having one of the most complete collections of old TV western and crime show music scores I have heard made working for him a real treat for me.

Musical scores of some of my favorite westerns like the "Magnificent Seven" have played with me sitting in a leather jacket and western hat while holding a red rider rifle across my lap. In my Walter Mitty mind, I was Yul Brynner exuding confidence, telling those bandits to get out of town or suffer the consequences. On another day I could be Nick Fury of the "Avengers," complete with eye patch and pistol in hand, trying to look menacing.

Illustration students drew or painted me in color while I sat absolutely still for 30 minutes at a time. My ability to sit still for long periods of time was one of the principle reasons David preferred me as a model, while another was my mustache. He loved that mustache displayed on the faces of his characters. He even told me if I ever shaved the mustache I was done as his favorite model. Then again I have heard that line from my wife many times over the years, so every time I think about a face change the voices in my head say, "You must stay who you are or the universe will collapse and it will be your fault."

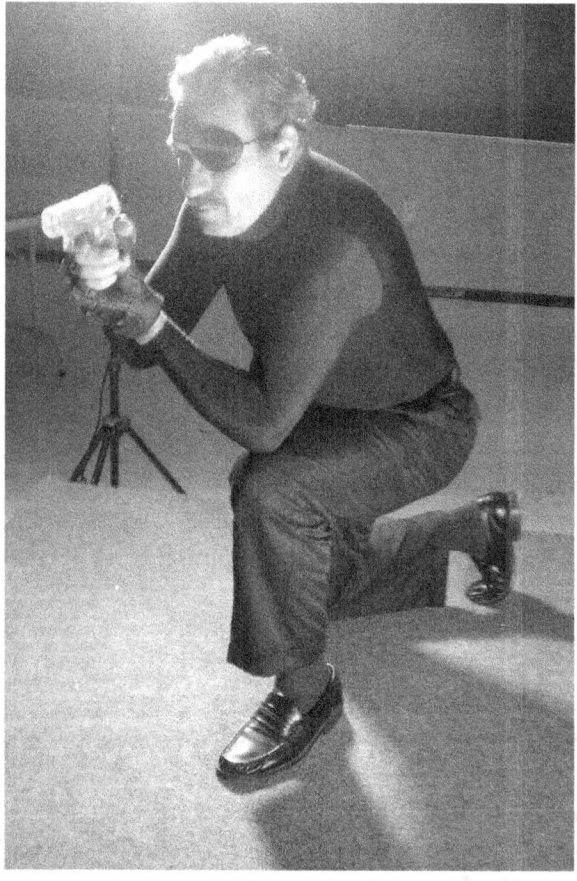

The Nick Fury look

Jenna is another instructor at the art institute with a flair for the dramatic and even the wacky at times. She would ask me first if the scene she wanted to draw would be something I'd be comfortable with and the asking is appreciated, but I don't think I ever said no to her. Yellow seems to be her favorite color, so I have worn a yellow jacket with matching rain hat and stood on a yellow ladder to be water colored for illustration. Even seated nude on a yellow colored see-through exercise ball helping to illustrate spheres. One of the wacky ones was stepping up a ladder with a foil dryer vent as a necklace and yellow yield street signs projected by light on my back in multiple diamonds making an abstract display with a nude figure in the middle .

My all-time favorite of wacky was done near Halloween. Jenna likes to do theme settings and Halloween is perfect for that. Ghosts, goblins and the macabre. On this occasion I was seated nude with a black cape around the back of my chair while holding a skull on my thigh and trying to look serious, even though it all was humorous to me. We had decided to repeat this pose a few times so a photo was needed to be able to adequately duplicate.

Quickly realizing that a skull on my thigh and genitals exposed would be beyond macabre and X-rated I moved the skull over my genitals and "voila," it's an R at worst, though kinky. We liked the new pose so much that we continued with it, which produced some very interesting Halloween drawings. Jenna is a great teacher and I liked the way she pushed the envelope to create interest for her students.

I have to say I get a big kick out of seeing the many different interpretations of myself drawn and hung on walls in the art schools. Dressed or nude it's always interesting to see just how different the students may represent you. The larger percentage of artwork I have modeled for are nudes however, and I got to thinking about just how many nude Steves are floating about the countryside, hanging on gallery walls, school hallways or hiding in closets. It was an educated guess but a scary one just the same when I figured it was pushing 30,000. That in itself would seem to make my figure public domain, which is not a term you should use when explaining to a spouse just what the job really entails. Perhaps one may want to consider that before taking a model position.

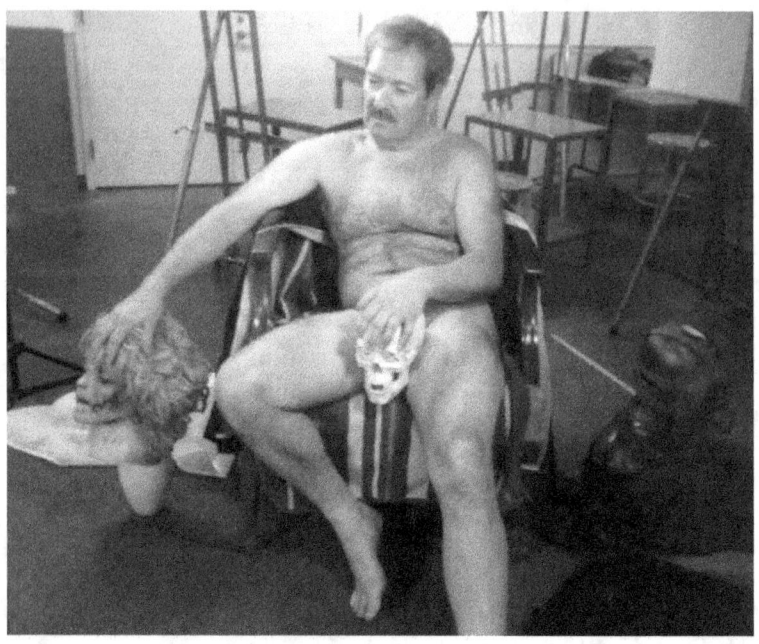

Scary Steve

Rising Star

It isn't easy for any college to make sure there will be a model available for every class that needs one. Models get sick just like everyone else or personal emergencies suddenly create a vacancy that may need to be filled on very short notice. I have had many calls to model for a class that has already started because a model did not show. I call it an "art emergency" when explaining to my wife why I had to rush out the door at 6:30 p.m. on a cold winter night with a bag in hand that she knows contains my action hero costume. Actually it has a robe, towel and slippers, and I really did keep it ready for just that occasion.

I think I know what a volunteer fireman feels like when the phone rings. "Steve, it's P.J. on the night desk at the art institute. Could you come over right now? Our model for tonight didn't show and you would be doing us a great favor if you could come over. You might think this would call for extra pay under the circumstances, but it doesn't." The institute knows I live closer than other models and can get there faster. Not to mention that I rarely say no even on a good TV night.

Finding good models is a constant task with most art schools, so on occasion they will run an ad in the local paper to see if they can find new, reliable and brave souls to try modeling. Few stay as long as I have, so consequently in the dual model situation used at the community college I get to work with quite a few different models. I would say I have made the acquaintance of a dozen other models. You might say working in the nude with other models would be a little more than making their acquaintance. Most certainly it is.

It gets really interesting when an ad is run for models because you just don't know who is going to respond and almost none have experience. This part makes it really fun for me because I get to make a new naked friend and pass along my years of nude wisdom to newbies that have no idea what they're getting into. The reasons they apply for such a job are really varied and I find their stories so very interesting.

Enter Liz, stage right. Jim had said he was expecting a new female model to come in and asked if I would mind if she came in during a class I was working. Some models prefer not to allow visitors for their own privacy. Let's face it, this is a members' club and not open to the general public. The art students understand the highly personal nature of figure drawing classes and the door is most often locked with a sign that asks guests to knock for entry. You might have guessed I am not one of those private model types and we could do this class outdoors for all I care. As it turned out Liz showed up just after I had finished a class and the students had left. I was on my cell phone as Jim gave her a tour of the studio while acknowledging my presence to her. We exchanged a knowing wave as I continued my call and she viewed all the drawings on the walls. My call kept me from any interaction at this point, but I was observing with curiosity the whole time. They did not stay long as Jim wanted to get to the interview process in his office down the hall.

I'm sure you have heard the saying, "don't judge a book by its cover" yet here I was trying to draw conclusions from the cover and no conversation at all. Very attractive, early 20s, blonde, shapely figure, black spandex pants, white blouse with just enough cleavage to accent her womanly form and I took this snapshot while on the phone in about 45 seconds. I think my intelligence analyst training kicked in for a minute.

Her carriage and seemingly confident nature told me she had modeling experience and she certainly did not flinch seeing all the nude art on the walls. Later, I stopped in to see Todd, our most competent art department coordinator, and low and behold here is Jim and Liz filling out employment forms. Wow, obviously no hesitation there, she is ready to give it a shot. Jim introduces me and we have a brief exchange, which lets me know she is coming to work real soon. In close proximity, I am getting a better look and confirming in my mind she is a confident young lady. She just walked into a college and said, "I'm here for that nude job you have."

It would be about a week before Liz and I got to work the same class, so there was some anticipation on my part as to how good a model she might be. There was more than equal anticipation on her part because as I found out later this was going to be her first nude model job and a whole new learning experience. Obviously the book cover judgment was incorrect. Now, as long as I have modeled, I must admit to curiosity with new models. It's just human nature.

We are on model stands about 15 feet apart at the start of our first class, so as Jim explains the lesson plan, we drop our robes to prepare. Now we are both nude and I am just looking at the floor. Well, I took a peek, of course. Liz has a great figure and takes a classic Italian pose so comfortably I thought she was a pro. Stunning classic form that made me want to grab my sketchbook and start drawing; like Leonardo I was thinking "Mama mia, I'ma gonna make a nice picture today." I knew then a new star was born in the art room and apparently the rest of the room did too, because only one student had an easel facing me .

It was just a few days later and only her third or fourth class that the lesson plan called for us to be on the same model stand. Liz was already in robe and waiting when I showed up for class, so I quickly changed and met her in the middle of the room. She then informed me we were going to work on the same stand. Okay then.

"Liz, you and me on the same stand?"

"Yes," she said, "the same stand." I'm trying so hard not to break out in the world's biggest smile, while being casual about it. There is no doubt in my mind this job is much better than being a door greeter at Wal-Mart. *Liz*, I thought, *this is baptism by fire for you today.*

All in all, it went very well. We were both very comfortable with no awkwardness.

Liz found the job while searching for something part time in the paper to add to her full-time job. She has a degree in psychology and was just trying to make a living like most of us. When in middle school Liz was not comfortable with her body and even through high school she did not get into the dating scene. It wasn't till college that she had a boyfriend that told her she was blessed with a great figure, and over time this began to boost her social comfort level. She feels great being appreciated and becoming part of art. I always tell models, "You are the art."

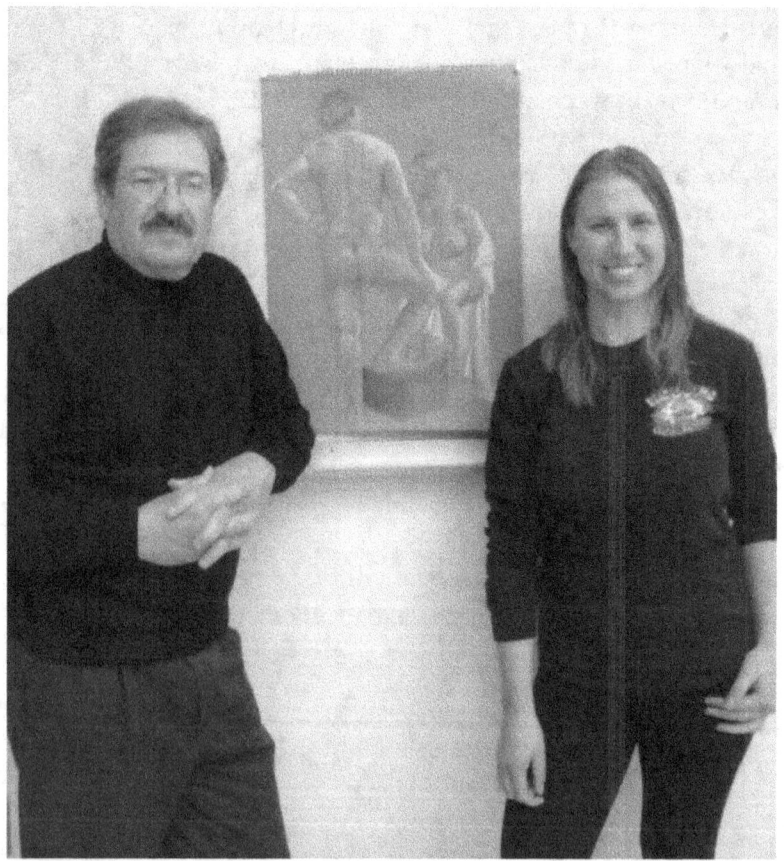

Liz and Steve

WHAT'S ON YOUR MIND

People often ask me, what do you think about when on the stand? It's a fair question, as the average class is three hours long, with the poses usually 20 minutes or more. You are trying to be as motionless as possible. This in itself presents many problems. I hate it when there is a pesky fly that thinks your nose is his private landing zone and no matter how you wiggle your nose, he just keeps coming back.

Then there's the itch that you can't figure out where it's coming from. You feel like a spider is crawling across your neck or just behind your ear. You twist your neck to one side to no avail. Then try raising your shoulder to scratch in behind the ear. Nothing works and it's very annoying. God forbid, it's the old scrotum itch or even worse are the hot summer days when you sweat. I have been in a body twist that places your armpits over your genitals when drops of sweat drip and fall on your penis or run down between your testicles and your thigh. You just sit there like nothing is wrong if you can stand it. If not, hey, this is a life drawing class.

Muscles often will go to sleep in a pose. You have to keep wiggling or making small adjustments to your pose, or you could actually fall down like I did in Chris's class. Your fingers can go numb or your back will ache and you just can't wait for the timer to go off so you can stretch out. In reality, if you have to move, no one is going to say a word. The teachers in particular do not want you in pain. It's hard enough to find nude models, so they don't want to scare any away.

My mind does drift often to places far away. In the beginning, you heard me say I was reliving Vietnam. I still have those thoughts and I can see it all clearly, almost like it was yesterday. The smells, or the dust or mud, depending on the season; the constant sound of gunfire on a daily basis. It becomes routine and surreal, but I still remember it.

On a happier note, I most often will think of my running races. You heard me speak of the different types of sport running I enjoy. Well, here is the connection. I love to plan race strategy. Some runners do, some don't. It's just my thing. So if I have a focus event coming up, I spend weeks in advance planning my race from the days of training to the actual race day. Often these are races I have done on the same course for many years, which give me the ability to see the entire course in my mind. I will plan where to accelerate and where to coast, and just how I expect to finish.

I can still recall vividly the 2006 National Snow Shoe Racing Championship at Bolton Valley, Vermont. It was my first national championship and I was plenty concerned. My friend Kermit and I drove over from New York just a few hours away and got a room the night before the race. We were both hungry in the early evening and I was really in the mood for a pizza. Here is where the phrase "don't do as I do, do as I say" comes in. Yep, very bad choice for me, a loaded pizza. I ate too much of it which made it even worse. Next morning I was still burping peperoni and Pepsi.

I felt like I needed a little kicker to get me started, so I got one of those energy drinks the kids like but come with warnings if you're over fifty or wearing a pacemaker. This turned out to be another disastrous choice. The gun went off and I hung near the back of the pack so not to get run over. This is a ten kilometer race on a ski mountain through mostly single track trails in the forest. After climbing for about a mile I was not only hyperventilating but getting chest pains, and my left arm was going numb. I actually stopped to check my pulse and see if it was over the red zone. Thinking I may be having a heart attack I slowed my pace to an even one and took my downhills easy to get my composure back. No, I did not consider stopping if that is what you were thinking.

I managed to survive, but finished way back in the pack. When on the model stand if you go off to dreamland and relive a moment like this one, it can actually show in your facial expression. Jed asked me one day if I was okay. He had noticed concern if not real sadness on my face. In truth he was right. I was having a moment of personal trauma that day and when I looked at his drawing, he actually had captured that look. It was amazing and I did not realize it myself until I saw his drawing.

One thing I have not mentioned is my powers of observation. My Army intelligence background teaches good observation skills. If I am not daydreaming I will certainly see you if you pick your nose, scratch your butt, unbutton your blouse or wear strong perfume. Never tease a naked man, ha ha, just kidding.

The bottom line is that everything in my life you have read about here has the potential to be in my mind when on the stand, even the writing of this book.

FUNNY STUFF

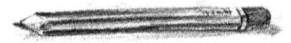

Y ou may have noticed by now this is not your average part-time job
and it is fraught with the most uncommon of situations which most
assuredly dictate adopting the Boy Scout motto, "Be Prepared."

One day I was in a reclining pose flat out on the model stand,
pillow under head and laying out on a sunny beach in a warm climate
with the sound of gulls nearby and a soft breeze over my body. I was
dreaming, of course, pretending it was true just to try to be comfortable,
and then the fire alarm goes off. A high pitched whistling sound that
makes you want to cover your ears rattles me out of my comfort zone
and up to a seated position. Jim tells everyone this is a test and directs
all to stop what they are doing and proceed to the door immediately.
No one seems to be concerned that the naked guy doesn't have time to
get dressed, as I grab my robe and file out at the end of the line. Jim has
that grin on his face like he is going to enjoy watching the spectacle of
the robed man with bare legs hanging out as he walks through hallways
following students down a staircase through a snack bar to the exit. As
I proceed down the stairs there are giggles from below as I realize some
are looking up my skirt with amusement. Teasing the art students that
see me all the time I blurt out, "No peeking," which of course brings
more laughter. Three sets of large double doors allows a mass exodus
of several hundred, most of whom have preceded me outdoors. It's an

early fall day but cool enough to tell me clothes would have been a much better option had I taken time to get them.

Naturally everyone outside turns around to face the building to see what is really going on. It is immediately apparent to me that I am walking into a huge reception of smiling faces, most of whom have no idea what goes on in the art studio. All those math and computer majors accustomed to running numbers through their expanding brains suddenly become dumbfounded at the site of a senior citizen in his bathrobe during a fire drill.

Now the *pièce de resistance*—Jim separates himself immediately and says, "You're on your own, pal." No one really wants to admit knowing me at this point. I can see small groups here and there staring at me, wondering what I am doing in a robe. Some I am sure are trying to guess if I am really naked under the robe. Admittedly, it is amusing if not confusing, but I am just trying to stay warm at this point and hoping the building is not really on fire. Fortunately it is not and after a few minutes we are allowed to return, with the milling process all over again and no one wanting to get too close to me.

I believe I have been through three of these all with no incident except laughter.

This model job has a curiosity about it for most people. The questions are varied of course, but a few come to me more often than others. One in particular is flatulence. I was quite surprised when one of my friends who is not only female but also an internationally acclaimed sports figure asked me about gas. "Steve, what do you do if you feel you're going to have a gas attack?" She is not the first one to ask this question, but it struck me as funny just because of who she is. We tend to put our heroes or celebrity favorites on a pedestal sometimes, but in reality they are all just people like the rest of us. They may have excelled at something and became famous but they still don't know how to fart gracefully while nude in a classroom.

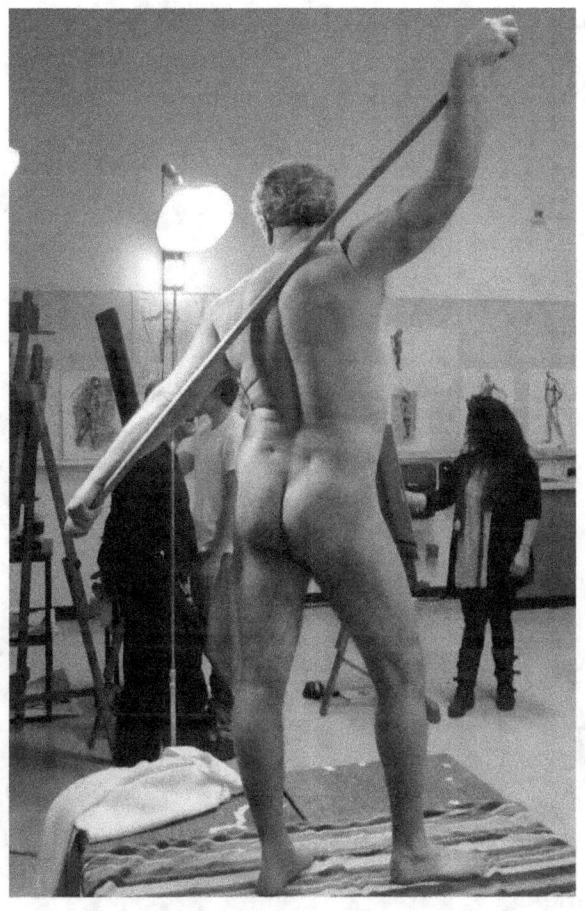

The answer to the question is painful at best. Tooting while nude in your bathroom is one thing, but in a classroom surrounded by curious young people, it is just not acceptable. I suppose they would all giggle, but I would surely blush with embarrassment. On one occasion I was having diarrhea at home and my stomach was very crampy. These are the days when you feel you should stay close to your own bathroom, but I never cancel on a class.

Well, here I was on the model stand and starting another series of cramps. The pain is mounting and I am wondering if I can stand it long enough to finish the timeframe of the current pose. Holding it in was so very painful. Maybe it's just gas and I could feel better by passing some just a little at a time. This could be disastrous under the circumstances, so I continue to hold. The pain just got too much to bear so I broke the pose with apology explaining I needed to take a break. Immediately stepping down, I grabbed my robe and ran out the door. Now there is a bathroom within the confines of the art department, but it's two right turns and a long hallway to get there. I am frequently seen in my robe in this area.

Walking as fast as I can while clenching my cheeks to avoid catastrophe, I finally get to the bathroom, which today felt like a lap around a quarter-mile track. There is only one stall in this room and you guessed it, someone is in there. The pain now is at red level 5 as I start to look at a wall urinal and wonder if I can get away with that. No, I just can't do it, so I go all the way back to the studio to put on my clothes because the next nearest bathroom is outside the art department and down another long hallway. I barely get into this bathroom which also has one stall but fortune favors the fearless this time. Now passing red level 7 on the pain scale, I rip the pants down and throw myself on the seat just in time for the inevitable explosion. Whew, I made it not a second too soon.

The day had just started, so I still needed to get through my classes on what would turn out to be one of the longest model days I ever had. Two more times I had to make that frantic run, hoping the next day's newspaper headline didn't read "hallway disaster at community college."

Thank goodness all this pain did not happen during a tour. Yes, I said tour. The art institute invites parents of prospective students to visit the school during class time to get a full perspective of teaching methods used. So in figure drawing or painting class a nude model would be in pose with the students rendering their perspective on the human figure when there is a knock at the door. I have had this happen to me several times and it never ceases to amuse me. The teacher answers the door and closes it again, then comes to me to ask my permission to allow a tour to walk through. I think it's nice they ask at least, but I always say yes because I know if I was the parent shelling out over $30,000 a year for my child's art school, I would want to know what they are getting for my money. On the other hand, maybe I am scaring them away. I am 69 years old, after all.

The tour enters, which may be a dozen or more parents and students. Now realize this may be their first exposure to a nude model because they don't do nude in high school art classes. I also agree to these tours because it is absolutely priceless to see the expressions on their faces. Dads don't want to look at me at all. If I were a female, I'm sure they would. Moms, on the other hand, are very interested. Students are mixed. I know some are thinking *Do I really have to do this to get an art degree?*

On one occasion I was on a break and walking the hallways in my bathrobe when I noticed some people entering the building. While I was previewing an exhibit in the student gallery some parents were filing in. Amused at my robe no doubt, there were curious looks. The executive director of the school came in to do a greeting before their tour, so I exchanged a hello with him and headed back to class. Sure enough a little while later there is the knock at the door and here they come. So here comes Steve—not me, the teacher is also named Steve— and one of my favorite teachers, asking me if they can pass through. The students always laugh when I say, "Sure Steve, I love tours," as I am sitting there nude. What struck me especially funny on that day was after the tour, about 20 minutes later, one of the moms came back and knocked again. Apparently she wanted to thank me personally for the permission to enter. Really now. Steve told her he would relay the message.

When I first met Steve I was new to the business and anxious to fit in, but not really sure what to do for impressing a teacher. I thought maybe some sports action poses might fit in for something different than traditional statue poses, so I brought a Frisbee with me. When I stretched out as to toss the Frisbee to my dog, I heard a resounding "Yessss," from Steve. Finally, a model who knows what to do. I didn't of course, but then all of a sudden I did because of his approval. So I kept on using the Frisbee in different ways, even the classic discus thrower. He then explained to me how many times he was frustrated with a model who stood like a tree, and every time Steve asked for a new pose he just got a different side of the tree. I have to thank him for giving me the vision to step out of the box once in a while to make the student draw the action, find the curves, the negative spaces and all those lines that make good composition.

Sizing Me Up

One of the lessons in figure drawing is a method of sighting the model. How do you perceive the model's size and proportion, and fit it to your page size? This method employs the use of sticks held at arm's length with one eye closed and your thumb as a marker to site particular parts of the body in relation to the whole body. So if you wanted to know how tall I was, you could site my head and then see how many heads tall I am. Okay, enough technical talk here.

Just envision you are asked to stand nude in front of 18 students in a semicircle about 10 feet away all pointing sticks at you, and then going up and down your body to locate areas to mark for reference. The teacher now hands me colored stick-on dots to mark these locations for further discussion. The first sticker usually is the middle of my chest, "now site between the nipples, class and find that spot." Mind you, I am placing stickers and listening to the teacher talk about my anatomy. Keep in mind I am a hairy Italian guy, so Jim in particular would take great humor in suggesting to the class we pull off a sticker to move to another spot.

Next the navel area and then the pubic mound. Oh no, we are not putting one there. Move to the hip instead, aahhh, much better. This process continues to the feet, all the while everyone is pointing the sticks and studying your body. So the next time you do shish kabab at your garden party, imagine all your guests pointing their sticks at you while you're cooking nude.

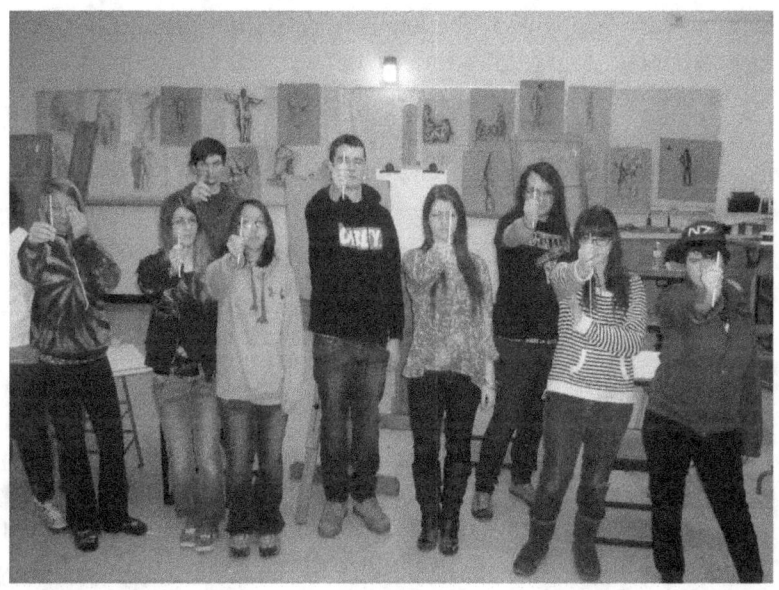

Sizing me up

My wife and I went to a concert one night at the community college. Tom Townsley and the Backsliders were playing. If you have never heard them, you really need to if you're a blues fan, especially if you like the harmonica, because Tom is just fabulous. We had a wonderful time. I had actually met Tom before at a drawing session as he is also an excellent artist.

On this occasion Pat and I were sitting up high in the theater; actually I think it was the same night I fell down the stairs, but that happened later. I had noticed one of the local artists that had drawn me several times sitting a few rows below. Sue had done a great drawing of me in a "dawn of the earth" setting. I was a primitive man sitting on a rock amidst the primordial soup. Well, among the many drawings Sue had of me there was one she hung in her bathroom. I'm not drawing any conclusions on that one, but it was very flattering.

I explained to Pat who Sue was (that was interesting) and told her I wanted to go say hello. This is all before the show. Sue had her boyfriend with her, whom I had never met, so an introduction was in order. "Hi, Sue," I said, "nice to see you."

Actually, Sue was one of the people telling me I should come see Tom perform. "Honey," she said to her boyfriend, "this is Steve, he is the guy hanging in my bathroom." Well, I just got "the look" from the boyfriend. You know what I mean by "the look?" You see the drawing of me in Sue's bathroom was a nude and every time he went to the bathroom at her house he got to see me. Wow, poor fellow.

New Students

Art students can often say the cutest things. Sometimes unknowingly, I'm sure. This next experience is just one of those. It was the beginning of a semester at the community college, which means all new students in the freshman classes, fresh from high school where nude models are not used for figure drawing. So it's an all new experience for them, which sometimes can make a funny day for me.

I walked into the art studio a little early that day, before Jim the teacher had arrived. Students often don't know what the teacher looks like on the first day, so I am often taken for the teacher by virtue of my age. This was the case when a female student asked me if I was the teacher and when I replied, "No, I'm the model." she got a surprised look on her face.

She then started to examine me from head to toe (and I'm still dressed) and states "Well excuse me sir if I stare, but I have never seen a naked man before." Isn't that just precious, I didn't know what to say.

At first I thought it was a joke, but I could see the look on her face was quite serious. I just told her that I was used to that and I was sure she would get used to it after the first few classes. In fact, a couple weeks later, her dad called from out of town to ask how college was going and one of her first comments was that she saw a naked man. Dad, not realizing that she was taking figure drawing, had the usual reply, "You what?"

"Dad, I'm taking art."

"Oh, okay" Dad replied, "and how was that for you?" She told him that the model was older than he was and she's doing fine.

I get a huge kick out of meeting the art students' parents. This has happened many times and it's just wonderful to see the look on their faces when the student says, "Mom, this is Steve, my model." Mom is now looking at me and trying to recall seeing me in her daughter or son's portfolio. In one case I was in an art gallery showing of student work with parents in attendance. As I walked around the show I ran into a female student with her mom standing near the students' drawings of me. The student introduced me to Mom as the model in the picture to which Mom said, "Oh, I have heard a lot about you, it's nice to meet you," as she compared me to the nude drawing on the wall.

On another occasion I was in one of my kitchen customer's homes when I noticed artwork on the wall. I asked whose work it was, since it seemed familiar to me and the missus said it was her daughter Amy's work, who had just graduated from the community college. I said, "Oh, is that Amy who works down at the steak house?"

"Why yes," was the reply, "do you know her?"

"Very well, in fact," was my reply.

"How do you know her?"

I looked at her and asked if she had seen a lot of Amy's classwork in drawing and as she started to say yes, she suddenly realized she had seen a lot of me in Amy's portfolio. "Ohhh, you're that guy in her drawings." She recognized me. It was priceless but also a statement to how good Amy had rendered me.

About a year before this in-home experience I was in the home of one of my running friends. Ingrid was a great middle-aged runner and always placed if not won her age bracket in most races she attended. I was doing Ingrid's kitchen also and when in the house one day her son Christian walked into the room. Ingrid introduced me to her son who looked a little familiar, but I could not place where I knew him from. However, Christian wore a big smile on his face as he said, "Hello Steve."

Ingrid said, "Do you know Steve?"

"Sure, he's my model from art class" Ingrid broke out in a big smile, saying that she was going to have to see Christian's portfolio now for sure.

At a summer art show I ran into the whole family again and while exchanging small talk with Ingrid and Dave, Christian comes along and blurts out how he likes the drawing of me in the gallery. Ingrid loves to tease me on this subject and indicates they are going into the gallery next to see Steve hanging on a wall.

My favorite parent-child experience was a Mom and daughter that were both in the same class. This was a new semester and I noticed three women in particular that seemed very friendly to each other. It turned out that they were all friends that went to the same church together. Kim was the youngest and often would make conversation at my breaks. She seemed very curious about how I got into the model business. Maryann and Donna were friendly as well and all seemed to have a good time with the class. It just seemed like I was missing something when they talked to me, like I was left out of the loop. One day, what I was missing was finally revealed. Maryann was Kim's mother and Donna was a very close friend. They were all church friends from a "born again" Christian church. Kim was actually a great singer and often did Christian concert solos.

Well, no one had told me for several weeks, so when I found out it just floored me. The Christian mother and daughter with a close friend, all drawing a nude man. The obvious question was, "How was this for the first-time art student, to be viewing a nude man with your daughter?" They admitted, they did not know whether to laugh or scream because they were probably expecting a female model the first time. It seemed to be a giddy experience for them but soon they got used to the experience and we all had a laugh over it.

Sometimes you wonder where the art work of your image may end up. This story really floored me. Cathy, a new next door neighbor, went to visit some friends. While at their house they were receiving some digital pictures via phone from a friend in Amsterdam, Holland. This friend was visiting the Anne Frank museum house, and sending pictures of her travels. One picture was a portrait that got Cathy's attention. She thought it was me, but how could that be? Showing the picture to her husband Ted and asking, "Does this look like Steve?"

Ted said, "Sure does," and in fact it was me. The friend sending the pictures was a former student at the art institute and added some of her own art in the mix. What are the odds that a drawing of me would be transmitted to my neighbor from a person in Holland? I don't know, but it sure was a hoot when she told me the story.

Once in a Wal-Mart, a female student introduced me to her whole family including Mom, Dad, brother and boyfriend. It was like a comedy, no one knew what to say except to smile. The boyfriend gave me the onceover, but not as much as Mom did. These situations remain an amusement to me no matter how many times they happen.

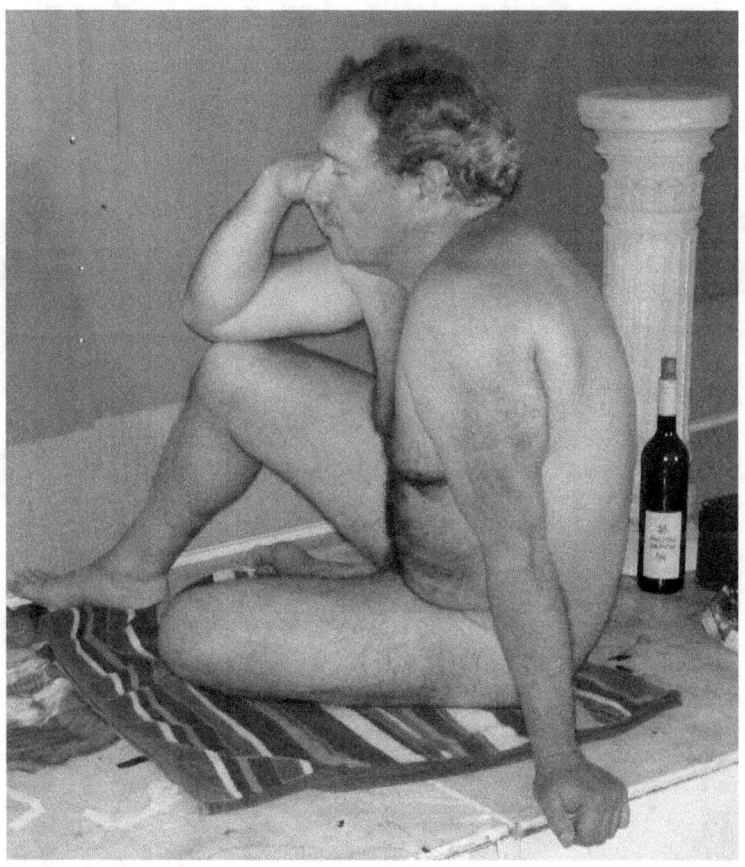

Seated Pose

MORE TEACHERS

Chris is the only guy I think I ever fell for. Don't jump to conclusions, let me explain. Chris was teaching a painting class at the art institute. Painting is a much slower process than drawing, so there will be one pose only for the entire three-hour class. Yes, I can take a break at my discretion, but care must be taken to be able to get back in the same pose position. On this occasion I was pretty new and again wanting to impress another teacher. So in fact I stood still in what was like a baseball batter position, but my bat was a 6ft long pole I was leaning on. This gave me a three-point stand and allowed for good balance and shifting to keep the blood moving in your legs. That is if you don't stay in pose too long. Well, every 20 minutes or so Chris would ask me if I would like to stretch, and me in my tough guy attitude said, "I'm fine thanks," and kept standing for 55 minutes with no motion.

What I did not realize was that my right leg had fallen asleep and was completely numb. There was no feeling at all. I was leaning so much on the pole that it was really all that was holding me up. Finally, Chris insisted we take a break and I let go of the pole to find I didn't have a leg to stand on (no pun intended). It was a weird feeling as I begin to fall, totally helpless, rotating my body to my backside as I headed for the floor, falling off a foot high platform to a tile-on-concrete floor.

Students gasped and exclaimed, "Oh noooo" and Chris running to my aid as I did a complete backwards 360 roll and landed upright on my butt. Friends, there is no way to fall gracefully when you are nude. It's just a fact. There I was, sitting on the floor with a leg that is sound asleep, so I can't even get up and Chris asking if he can do anything, but at more than arm's length from the naked man. I had him get my robe for warmth and I sat there for a while rubbing the sleeping leg. Fortunately, all that physical stuff I did kept me from being injured except for my pride, and after a short break we were able to continue. Taking more frequent breaks, of course.

Chris is a great teacher and I enjoyed working many of his classes over the years in both painting and drawing.

Annette also was teaching at the institute, often doing evening community arts classes. She was the first female teacher I would model for and admittedly I was very nervous about that. Here was a mature woman closer to my age than the students', who would be pointing to my body for illustration. Probably my fears were the same as having a female doctor. Men generally are not comfortable with that, but as my wife points out, "Now you know how women feel going to a male doctor." Annette quickly put me at ease with her teaching style and my fears were relieved.

Community arts classes invite the public in general to hone their drawing skills. This means all ages and levels of skill may attend. Now for me the model this opens the door to meeting people from all walks of life, even someone you may know, including your next door neighbor. Well, I haven't had that happen yet, but pretty close.

During breaks from the drawing I have the opportunity to view their work and meet the artists. One night there was an excellent artist just practicing his skills and during our conversation I discover he was an advertising guy and illustrator. So I asked him if he knew my neighbor Bob and sure enough, they had worked together early in their careers at the same ad agency. What a small world.

The meeting that really got me laughing though was my grandson's third grade teacher. Yup, she was a practicing artist and when I asked what she did and she said teacher, I inquired where, and it turns out to be the same school my grandchildren go to. So I ask if she knows any of the four that go there, and sure enough, one is in her class. So now envision the look on her face when I show up for school activities, including the several times I have been a chaperone on bus trips to the zoo, etc. Seeing your student's grandfather nude just has to be off the chart for an elementary school teacher.

Ken was also a teacher at the art institute. Some teachers are so very much into the students drawing correctly that they go from one to the next, offering helpful suggestions and completely lose themselves and the fact that there is a model in the room. Ken is one of those teachers. I call it being diligent to a fault. Now I can't fault him for being diligent because he really is a great teacher and has the students' best interest at heart.

Models are usually working on a timer so they can plan their pose based on difficulty and perhaps what the next pose will be. However, most teachers do not have a timer so they casually watch the clock on the wall. This frequently leads to the model being in pose longer than they need to be. I started carrying my own timer just for those occasions.

On more than one occasion Ken would be go around doing his usual critique, and then look at the clock to realize just how long he had been teaching. It's then that I get the apology.

"Sorry, Steve, I forgot how long you have been standing there."

"Gee Ken, it's not a problem, just give me a few minutes to get the blood back in that leg that fell asleep."

The fact is that quite a few teachers do this, so I don't really mean to pick on Ken. I haven't worked for a teacher I did not like and Ken is no exception there, either. The institute is lucky to have him.

Jed teaches at the community college and has earned a place in my teachers' hall of fame for creative poses. Second-year students get to hone their skills with more intricate work, including two models in the same picture. The use of a theme or storyline often taken from Greek mythology adds to the complexity, as well as to the fun of being a model. It was Jed who first introduced me to these intricacies, which made the end of the semester more than worth waiting for. First, of course, I get to play a scene with all the nice ladies I have mentioned here. It's very satisfying to see yourself in a work of art that often will make a gallery show and be on display for as much as a month. I am inconsequential to the art, but take great pride in putting in what energy I have, hoping to inspire the artist. Working the energy with a partner is so vital to the storyline that I feel like an actor on stage.

One of my favorite stories was the death scene played by Stephanie. Even though there was humor in it for both of us working so closely, there was still sincerity in the theme that made it a great picture. I believe we did that pose for three classes, which was nine hours total time. Jed was drawing this one himself and that drawing remains one of my favorites. Right at the end he decided to draw a knife in his picture, laying between Stephanie and me, leaving the question to the viewer: did she commit suicide or did he murder her? I was portraying remorse in viewing her dead body, which still leaves the viewer to decide. Kudos to Jed. The illustration in the Stephanie chapter is similar to the pose in Jed's drawing. The female model is my friend Cassandra, who models at another college.

Jim is the guy who hired me for the community college for which I am thankful as it has been a very rewarding experience. I don't always appreciate his music choice, but the classic cello sound makes great mood for the serious pose. Many students bring their own music, rendering it kind of a moot point for them.

I have worked with many teachers, all of whom I think are great, but I have spent the most time with Jim. It makes me wonder if I should approach colleges to get paid for doing teacher critiques. In all sincerity, I have to say Jim is one of those people who makes you want to be a teacher. His approach to students is almost as a family member. Getting them to realize their dedication and personal motivation are the things that will take even an average artist to a rewarding career in an art-inspired field.

Jim also has a quick wit and sense of humor, which helps keep some brightness on a gray day, even if he does borrow jokes from me.

STUDENT VIEWS

I am always interested in the student response to figure drawing. Art is taught in many different forms. Figure is just one, but certainly essential if they are going to be working in an art career. Illustration, advertising, marketing, and comic books all have people forms in them.

Many may not think of this when they start in their art education, so the first-time nude figure class may be somewhat of a surprise. The student over the course of four years will take many figure classes in both drawing and painting, as well as illustration. Consequently, they will be exposed to many different models of both genders and wide age difference. The responses are varied of course, just as personalities are. The following is one of my favorites, coming from a former student.

Sara, in her own words.

The first art class I had with a nude model (that I can recall) was actually with you. I was a bit nervous at the beginning of the very first class. One factor that might have contributed to a slight feeling of nervousness/ awkwardness was the fact that it was a mixed gender art class, and all of the students were around 18–23. It's an age where most people are exploring their sexuality in college, and it's impossible to ignore the fact that there is something innately sexual about a nude body. The only thing I found funny was the fact that I was nervous, because I wasn't sure where that feeling was coming from.

I think that, to some extent, seeing another person naked reminded me of insecurities I had with my own body. That is a very personal thing, and those classes were cathartic in that they forced me to look at the individual uniqueness of the models. What makes a good piece of art, in my opinion, is capturing the beautiful imperfections of each individual. No one body is perfectly symmetric, from our arms and legs down to the hairs that make up our eyebrows.

Coming into that first class, I probably expected a young female model, because most of the nudes that I've seen feature young women. But to be honest, it wasn't my first time seeing a nude man, so that in itself wasn't particularly shocking. It probably would have been shocking if it was. I might not have even signed up for the class! I haven't had to adjust in the same way to the presence of a nude female model.

There is also a huge difference between looking at a picture of a nude versus being in the same room with a nude person. It's a much more powerful presence. It's incredible how the body has been sexualized to such a degree in our society that it has the ability to create such discomfort and awkwardness. It's something I'm very glad I've gotten over. That art class helped. You helped. Thanks for that.

Once I started drawing, I was too busy focusing on the intricacies of my art piece to be nervous. It became all about the details: muscle tone, shadows, depth perception, the curve of the model's back. I also like listening to my iPod when I draw, music helps keep me "in the zone."

Your age was a factor in the sense that it allowed me to work with certain details that I hadn't experienced drawing before. Specifically, the tone of the skin, the fall of the hair, the way your expression changes the shading of your face. It's different than it would be when drawing a child, or an old man (there was a compliment in there for you!). It didn't bother me, and there was nothing negative in it for me. It was just a unique element for me to work with. There is a great value in working with models of different ages and both genders because it forces me even more to see the person as *they are, rather than replicating the same young woman in different poses, for example.*

I love that you fell asleep during the resting pose! We got an extra 10 minutes of drawing in! I think it's funny you don't remember it.

I've always been impressed with the model's ability to stay still for so long and take direction so well. Kudos.

Since I've been away, I've actually gone to a few more life drawing sessions. My experience here has been relatively the same, and the model has always been the same man. I hope to keep doing it, as I get so much out of it.

Cheers,
Sara

I think Sara's candor here was stellar, expressing true feelings that often are difficult for me to get from current students. I could not phrase this any better, even with countless interviews. Thank you, Sara.

The Naked Truth

The models I have written about each have had a different reason to become a model. Some are personal and others just needed a job. One in particular sticks out above the rest. I haven't spoken about Amanda till now. She remains one of the top picks for my "nude model hall of fame." She had heard about modeling through a friend and found it curious. Having one job already, she could use more income while still seeking her true career path goal.

Amanda was very thin, probably the thinnest model I ever worked with, yet she had a shape that was graceful and a talent to fall into poses with ease that made for great drawing. Her face had a haunting nature to it that compelled me to draw her myself. I did so on a several occasions.

We had a serious chat one day that revealed one of her component reasons for taking the job. I was so taken by her story that I won't ever forget it. Amanda admitted to having an eating disorder and apparently being ill for some time as a result. In recovery mode one's mental state can be most important. She chose modeling to test public acceptance of her figure, and hopefully raise her self-esteem. I just sat and thought *Wow, that is really deep.* She put her nude figure on display in seeking acceptance of who she was. The equally interesting part is that it actually worked. Her self-confidence actually grew, she became very comfortable with the nudity and really enjoyed the job. We worked together for a year and I was so very glad to have made her acquaintance. She did find her chosen career job and left the area, but we have talked a couple of times since.

One of my dear model friends was a former student at the community college. Cassandra as a student was always sporting a smile when I came in the classroom and openly engaged me in conversation. She was always a glowing light in the room for me. After she graduated she went on to a four year college and continued in art. It was at this college that she decided to try her hand at being a model. I was an inspiration to her, or so she told me.

Cassandra did a lot of growing up on her own as a teenager. She wasn't really comfortable with her own body and her maturing stages into a young woman became a trip of personal discovery. It was this process that gave her the confidence to try being a model. She had told me her comfort level to be nude in a class didn't really come until after her first intimate encounters with a boyfriend. Obviously her ability to share this with me indicates the connection we shared in our interest in art and as friends. I was so very happy she offered to help me with the book by posing for two of the illustrations you see here.

Hannah was a full-figured gal and a student at the community college. Like Devon she could not model there as a current student. She came to me as Devon did, to ask where she might model, but her reasons were different. First it was for a job, students always need money. Her inquiry though was concern for her full figure. She wondered if her size would be a deterrent to hiring. I assured her that size didn't matter, and promptly made a referral for her at the art institute. The only real concern is if you can you stand still for long periods of time. Hannah did get a job at the institute and they love her "Rubenesque" shape.

For me the job is downright exhilarating. There is always something new happening and I never get bored. As a part-time job I don't think I could be any happier somewhere else. I have learned a lot about art and continue to grow with it and I absolutely love to draw. To observe and draw from live models is one of the greatest challenges you could have, and to be the life model gives every appreciation of how difficult it is for the artist.

I have made many friends among both faculty and students, which has enriched my life immensely. No matter what age you are, should you have the time, inclination or the need for part-time work and you would like to step out of the box, then I suggest you inquire with local colleges to see if this is available to you. It might just be that turn in the road you were looking for.

ABOUT THE AUTHOR

Steve was born and raised in Utica, NY, where he attended local schools. He graduated high school from Utica Free Academy in 1962. Steve interrupted his college years to join the U.S. Army where he was recognized with the Bronze Star while serving as an Intelligence Analyst in Vietnam. After Vietnam Steve was able to use the G.I. bill to finish his business management degree from Mohawk Valley Community College in 1973.

Steve loves the outdoors, especially fishing, jogging and cycling, or just watching the stars go by. He has been married to his wife, Patricia for 45 years and has two children and six grandchildren. He counts himself a lucky man to have such a great family.

Late in life he found this part time job as a figure model for art schools and fell in love with the art. Now besides being a model Steve is also learning to draw. This is what inspired him to write the book.

www.ingramcontent.com/pod-product-compliance
Lightning Source LLC
Chambersburg PA
CBHW071320220526
45468CB00001B/442